# 301

## GREAT
## IDEAS FOR

# SELLING
# SMARTER

*from America's*
## Most Innovative Small Companies

### INTRODUCTION BY DON PEPPERS

#### EDITED BY TERI LAMMERS PRIOR
#### WITH JACQUELINE LAPIDUS

Like its four predecessors in *Inc.*'s "301" series, this book would not have been possible without the input and cooperation of some of the most energetic, responsive, and optimistic people we as writers and editors could hope to encounter. I refer to the hundreds of company owners, managers, and sales executives who responded to our calls, followed up our requests for information, and shared their stories. To each of them, we express a sincere thank-you.

Thanks also go to my husband, Shawn P. Prior, who, as a seasoned sales manager himself, not only contributed one of his own trade secrets but also made perceptive observations that helped identify the smartest ideas from well over 300 companies. Much appreciation also goes to Cregan Montague, my editorial assistant, and Sara Fraser, my assistant editor, who became stalwarts in the early stages of researching and editing this book.

I also appreciate the efforts of the original writers and reporters for *Inc.*, the source of more than half of the items in this book. Susan Greco, who has covered selling and marketing for the magazine for the past five years, deserves extra credit since so many of the stories originated in her columns. Indeed, the book would not have been possible without the editors and writers who produced *Inc.* magazine in 1996 and 1997: Margherita Altobelli, Marc Ballon, Alessandra Bianchi, Leslie Brokaw, Leigh Buchanan, Bo Burlingham, Christopher Caggiano, John Case, Susan Donovan, Donna Fenn, Jay Finegan, Jill Andresky Fraser, George Gendron, Stephanie Gruner, Phaedra Hise, Michael Hofman, Michael Hopkins, Joshua Hyatt, Nancy Lyons, Joshua Macht, Robert Mamis, Martha Mangelsdorf, Cheryl McManus, Evelyn Roth, Sarah Schafer, Jeffrey Seglin, Thea Singer, Jerry Useem, Edward O. Welles, and Stephanie Zacharek.

Thanks also go to the *Inc.* Business Resources (IBR) staff, whose professionalism, support, and enthusiasm carried us through the inevitable glitches engendered by producing a book of this scope: managing editor Gail Anderson, who assembled the pieces and "kept count;" copy editor Audra Mulhearn, who polished the prose; fact-checkers Robina Gangemi and Simeon Ketchum, who diligently verified the details from each source; designer Cindy Davis, who gave the book its readable look; Joe Durand, Leslie Graham, Lynette Haggard, Kevin Levesque, and Kimberly Scott, who oversaw the myriad production details; and product director Jan Spiro, who served as coach, sounding board, and business manager.

Finally, special recognition goes to Jacqueline Lapidus, whose knack for wordsmithing helped shape the early drafts; and to Bradford W. Ketchum, Jr., editorial director of IBR, who gave me the opportunity to produce this newest entry in the "301" series. His constant search for excellence is deeply appreciated.

—*Teri Lammers Prior*
*Marblehead, Mass.*

Editor's note: *Teri Lammers Prior served as a reporter and staff writer for* Inc. *magazine for nine years, during which she earned national recognition for her "Hands On" management columns.*

# The Power of Positive Listening

**O**nce upon a time, there was a young man who began his career as a sales clerk in his neighborhood hardware store. He paid careful attention to every detail, and he had a winning way with customers, remembering them each by name. Over time, he worked his way up through the ranks, eventually taking over the store. Soon he launched another store, and then another, until he presided over a whole chain of successful hardware stores. But even though he became a very prosperous store owner, it was his habit to continue clerking one day a week in the original neighborhood store where he had started. So every Saturday morning his neighbors could still find him right there, now a successful, wise old master salesman.

One Saturday morning, a young boy came in and asked if he could use the phone. "Sure, Jimmy," the man said generously, pointing to the phone. So Jimmy picked up the phone, pulled a piece of paper out of his pocket, and dialed a number he had written on it. The wise old salesman was able to overhear what was apparently this young boy's sales pitch:

"Hi, Mrs. Wilson, I'd like to cut your lawn this summer. I think I can do a great job for you, and I'd just like to stop by and discuss it…Oh, someone's already cutting your lawn?…OK, but are you really happy with what they're doing for you?…Right, well, I'm glad you have someone right now, but could I call you again at the end of the summer, and if you aren't happy then, maybe I could cut your lawn next year?…OK, Mrs. Wilson, I'll call you toward the end of September, thanks."

At the conclusion of the conversation the boy folded the paper with the number on it, put it in his pocket, and started out the door. It was obvious that this was the only number he was going to call with his pitch, and the master salesman just couldn't stand it. His heart went out to the boy.

"Jimmy, Jimmy, wait a minute. Listen, son, I've been a salesman all my life, and I can tell you your pitch was great, really a great sales pitch. This prospect didn't buy it, but so what? Selling is also about numbers, Jimmy, and you only called one prospect. The more people you try to sell to, the more you'll sell, I guarantee it. If you were to use that pitch on 10 prospects instead of just one, I'm willing to bet you'd be mowing five or six more lawns tomorrow!"

But Jimmy quickly shook his head. "I wasn't trying to cut Mrs. Wilson's lawn, sir," he replied. "I've been cutting her lawn for four weeks already. I just wanted to make sure she's happy with the job I'm doing."

As the young lad turned to leave the store, the old master was left wondering which one of them was actually the smarter salesman.

A smart salesperson knows that no sale is ever final. There is always hope for another sale, even if you've been locked out of this one. And if you're lucky enough to make a sale this time, you can count on the fact that someone, somewhere, will be trying to undo it, just as you would try to undo theirs. The only way to ensure that a sale remains sold is to ensure that the customer remains satisfied with the merchandise.

But what exactly is it that satisfies a customer? In the end, that's a totally subjective question, because one customer's complete satisfaction is another's marginal service. Each customer is different, and treating different customers accordingly is the essence of smart selling. Selling smarter means getting to know a particular customer's needs and then selling to that customer as an individual. Smart selling is focused always on the "you" and not on the "me" of the sales transaction.

If there's one recurring theme that runs through *301 Great Ideas for Selling Smarter*, it is that the smart salesperson is *you*-oriented, not *me*-oriented. Over and over again, in reading through this book, you'll see how smart salespeople profit by relying on their knowledge and understanding of customers. Truth is, it's not the easiest thing to be you-oriented. Many of us in sales have succeeded on the strength of our intelligence, our winning personalities, and our ability to express ourselves well, both on paper and on our feet. Listening skills are not always at the top of the list of natural talents for an otherwise accomplished salesperson.

But a really ambitious salesperson also knows that there's no faster way to become smart at selling than by developing a talent for listening to customers. So the smart salesperson finds more reasons to listen, literally seeking out more occasions to interact with a customer and obtain insight. Selling smarter means listening smarter. The smart salesperson concentrates on what he or she learns from the customer—focusing on that customer's individual needs—so that with every sales call the salesperson becomes even more you-oriented.

In the end, there's no substitute for knowing who's across the desk or on the other side of the conference table. There's no better way to make a sale than knowing that person's individual preferences and needs. Putting yourself in your customer's shoes, sitting in your customer's own chair—this is the essence of selling. And the better you are at doing this—the better you are at listening to your customer and understanding him or her individually—the smarter you'll be at selling.

*Don Peppers, a partner at Marketing1to1/Peppers and Rogers Group, in Stamford, Conn., is the author of* Life's a Pitch Then You Buy.

# I

"The key is to have some kind of system for rating prospects. Then, as the ratings change, you can shift your resources to those deals that have the greatest chance of closing. That, in turn, leads to the ultimate payoff: more control of the selling process and more accurate sales forecasts."

**TOM COLBY**
vice-president of sales,
Campbell Software, Chicago

# 1
## IDEA

# Hundred-Dollar Drive

**H**aving difficulty making yourself stand out at a big trade show? Here's an example of a guy who took to the streets right outside the show to get his business rolling.

Unable to wrangle a booth at his first major computer-industry show, Ken Hawk, CEO of 1-800-BATTERIES, targeted customers in taxicabs. Hawk promoted his rechargeable-battery business by **enlisting local taxi drivers to hand out catalogs** to any passengers who were going to or coming from the nearby trade show.

To obtain the drivers' cooperation, some of the company's employees acted as "mystery riders" and awarded a $100 bill to every cabby who gave them a 1-800-BATTERIES catalog. Four drivers won, and the word got around.

Hawk says the unconventional marketing effort generated 275 orders worth $14,794 in sales. "We spent $400 and got some great exposure that we couldn't get any other way," he says. Now he can get into the shows—and his company in Reno, Nev., is clocking $16 million.

# For Everything a Season

If you're competing with a pack of companies in an overcrowded market, discovering an overlooked niche is like getting a breath of fresh air. Ed Fitzsimmons Jr., president of Yellowbird Motorlines, knows this for a fact.

In 1994, Fitzsimmons was driving along the road near his company's headquarters in New Bedford, Mass. He looked out the car window and saw cranberries—acres and acres of them. While New England produces a whopping one billion pounds of cranberries annually, just a handful of trucking companies serves this burgeoning market. Many aren't willing to **go the extra mile to serve a seasonal market** because it seems so difficult. It requires hiring temporary drivers, securing extra equipment, and having a dispatcher on duty 24 hours a day, seven days a week. Fitzsimmons found, however, that it's worth the investment, because these farmers are willing to pay a premium to have their valuable, time-sensitive, and perishable freight delivered promptly.

Fitzsimmons calls on the cranberry farmers during the spring and begins planning for their fall harvest needs eight weeks before the projected harvest date. He grew the family-owned business to $8 million in sales in 1997 and has secured other seasonal work to even out his schedule: blueberries in summer and lumber in winter.

# Territorial Imperative

**S**ince 1995, founder Alan Newman has built the Magic Hat Brewery, in Burlington, Vt., into a multimillion-dollar operation that sells more than 15,000 barrels of beer a year. He does it by staying close to home—despite his long-term goal to sell nationally.

"Marketing, selling, and actually shipping goods in hundreds of different directions can easily overwhelm a fledgling enterprise," Newman explains. "It's less intoxicating but more realistic to **take on one small territory at a time**." Newman chooses a state or metropolitan area, waits for sales to reach a saturation point, then moves into a neighboring territory. He also keeps prices steady. Magic Hat beer is delivered, sold, and consumed in four New England states. Newman adds, "We are building sales by building a brand."

4

**IDEA**

# Permits in the Pipeline

**B**reaking into a new territory often requires obtaining government approval—a Byzantine process that can hold up sales. To help speed up entry into a new market, Infiltrator Systems, in Old Saybrook, Conn., has its sales representatives **call on the environmental regulators that issue permits for the company's systems**.

"We try to find out what makes the program in their area tick, what their beliefs are about how septic systems work, and what their problems are," explains Roy Moore, vice-president of manufacturing.

To adequately address regulators' needs, sales representatives go through an intensive training course. Engineer Randy May spends time with representatives in the field so that they can learn the basics of installation procedures. They also travel with more experienced salespeople and visit regulators with them. "We don't expect them to be effective for six months to a year," says Moore. "It's a big investment." But it brings in big returns: Infiltrator Systems' sales topped $60 million in 1997.

**5**

**IDEA**

# Tapping New Age Culture

**N**ew market trends wrought by generational differences are causing business upheavals. Generational preferences are spawning new products and services at warp speed and causing old ones to disappear, according to J. Walker Smith and Ann Clurman, authors of *Rocking the Ages* (HarperBusiness, 1997, $25, 800-242-7737). Paying attention to age-related marketing may give you a key competitive advantage in the marketplace.

Smith and Clurman, who are partners at a demographic research firm called Yankelovich Partners, in New York City, say that **targeting a specific generation for a sales campaign** can be even more effective than targeting demographic criteria such as income, gender, and education. "Don't assume that because your customers are turning a certain age they will behave in the same way as those who came before them," Smith and Clurman warn. Many housing developers, for example, are discovering that Baby Boomers are far less interested in cookie-cutter retirement communities than were their elders. Knowing how the motivations of your customers are tied to the underlying values of the generation to which they belong will help you tailor your products and services to their needs, interests, and desires.

Also, say Smith and Clurman, avoid "generational myopia," or short-sighted application of your own generation's values and attitudes to strategies for marketing to another generation. To sell to a particular age group, find out what else people in that generation are buying, and why. For openers, conduct a search of Internet newsgroups via Deja News (www.dejanews.com). The super-search tool can give you insights on attitudes and trends around the world.

# 6
**IDEA**

## Escape Artist

In his zealous attempt to jump-start sales of Sunfish/Laser, Peter Johnstone embarked upon an ambitious plan to update the venerable Sunfish sailboat. Along the way, he discovered that it made more sense to design a completely new boat. "The Sunfish was too expensive, too difficult to learn, and tippy in the water," says Johnstone, who dubbed his new craft the Escape.

For one year Johnstone tried to sell both models. However, it was difficult for his sales force to jeopardize customer relationships, which were built on the old core product, by aggressively selling the new product. And boat dealers didn't seem to care for the new, smaller Escape. However, outdoor recreation dealers, in search of the next sea kayak, were enthusiastic.

Since his small company couldn't afford a sales force for each market, Johnstone decided to jump ship. He **sold the old company to keep it from slowing sales of his new product**, and he focused all his energies on the new company, Escape Sailboat Co., located four doors down the hall. Sales have, well, billowed. In 1997, the Portsmouth, R.I., company sold 1,800 Escape sailboats and is on track to sell 3,400 in 1998.

# 7
**IDEA**

# Shall We Link?

**E**lliott Rabin, president of Ridout Plastics, a $10-million company in San Diego, wanted to make sure his Web site would generate traffic—and business. So he **enlisted another Web site with an established traffic pattern as his partner**. The *San Diego Source*, an electronic financial newspaper, is a hot spot for locals. Web surfers can click straight through to Ridout's site from the *Source*'s technology page, which Ridout sponsors.

Rabin uses DigitalStyle's WebSuite, a collection of Web-authoring tools, to design and ship the pages himself—so that he has total control over their content and appearance without the hassle or cost of maintaining a server. He also spends about five hours a week searching the Web for complementary sites to link up with. When he finds a good fit, he e-mails the organization to ask if it would be interested in linking to Ridout's site. He has established links with several universities, including Cornell, which has a plastics department.

Through partnering on the Web, Rabin has made Ridout *the* plastics site. He even plans on scanning his company's entire corporate research library into its Web site to help researchers. Even if people don't buy right away, he says, "they might come back to buy, or they might tell other people to come to our site because we're known as plastics experts." In fact, 25% of Ridout's new business comes from people whose first encounter with the company was on the Web.

Ridout's site now gets 12,000 to 15,000 hits a month. Its overseas sales have expanded into six new countries, and sales have grown considerably, increasing 50% in custom-designed brochure holders alone.

# The Name's the Game

**Y**ou have only one chance to make a good first impression, and the name of your company may be the way you do it. "Be choosy," advises marketing guru Jack Trout, president of Greenwich, Conn., marketing consultancy Trout & Partners Ltd. "Remember, **the best names are locked directly to a product benefit or selling proposition**." Here are Trout's comments on some company names, in light of his own selling strategies.

~ *Simply describe what you're selling.* Your name is the first thing consumers know about you, so convey the idea in very literal terms, as Toys 'R' Us did. Guiltless Gourmet is memorable, and it tells you the product is both tasty and healthy.

~ *Connect the name with the strategy.* A descriptive name like Lens Express tells consumers that the company is offering speedy contact-lens services. While it isn't exactly clever, a name like that can be effective if a company slogan defines it further—say, by promising delivery within a certain time frame, as Federal Express did with "absolutely, positively overnight."

~ *Use specific rather than generic names.* Having a big idea with a catchy name isn't enough. The Kitchen Works, for instance, sounds more like a welcome-to-the-club name. To compete, you have to give customers a sense of why they are going into this store instead of someone else's.

~ *Allow for expansion.* Musical Chairs Ticket Service focuses solely on music, so it may not help you sell tickets to sports events as well. While a clever name is important, it has to line up with the company's strategy.

**9**

**IDEA**

# Add Our Product and Stir

**W**hile the Young Pecan Co. sells nuts by the trailer truckload to major food manufacturers, its sales reps are more likely to be chatting up a recipe developer than a purchasing agent who's barraged by calls from competitors. That's because **what's happening in research and development labs sometimes offers the best sales opportunities**.

At this early stage of the game, Young's sales reps can help create a pecan-packed ice cream for Häagen Dazs or a nuttier breakfast cereal for Post. Working with the R&D labs is harder than simply quoting a price over the phone to a buyer, but it helps the company maintain its relationship with major food manufacturers.

"To create the breakfast cereal for Post, we had to build a piece of equipment to apply a preservative to the nuts," says J. Givens Young, founder and chairman. He adds that such specialized equipment is another barrier to entry for a competitor.

In addition to getting in on ground-floor opportunities, working with the R&D lab also insulates a company from the risks of dealing with buyer turnover in the purchasing department. "It seems that buyers change about every two years, so it's important to have multiple contacts within an organization to support your company," advises Young, who founded his Florence, S.C., business in 1942 and has grown it from the smallest pecan processor out of 150 to the largest of just 22 still in business.

# 10
## IDEA

• GENERATING LEADS •

# Rewiring Auto Motives

**S**elling cars has always been a commission-based business that encourages the salesperson to strip the customer's wallet. Pete Ellis, founder of the Internet's first and biggest Web-based automotive site, hated traditional car dealerships with salespeople waiting to jump on the next customer who walked in the door. Ellis's vision of a new way of selling cars is actually changing the auto industry.

Ellis's business, Auto-By-Tel (ABT), in Irvine, Calif., **uses the Web as a referral service to introduce highly qualified prospects to a national network of dealers** that have signed exclusive contracts with ABT. Ellis makes money, not by taking commissions on the cars bought by ABT users, but by charging dealers for access to those buyers. In return, dealers get more sales, lower transaction costs—as much as 75% lower than the cost of a traditional "walk-in" sale—and lower advertising costs. The Web leads are motivated, highly educated people who know what they want. The pressure is off the salespeople, too, which makes everybody happier when the deal is done.

**11**

**IDEA**

# Customers in Orbit

**P**rospecting for customers has entered the space age. Satellites orbiting the earth at four miles per second are equipped with digital cameras so sharp that they can pick out individual towels on a beach. Archadeck, a fast-growing $25-million home-add-on franchiser headquartered in Richmond, Va., **uses information gathered by these geographic information systems (GIS) to help target new customers**. In 1994 the company began managing its direct-contact marketing campaigns with GeoWizard, a GIS "prospect finder" produced by GeoDemX Corp. (810-569-3939).

Archadeck used to try to drum up business the old-fashioned way—hanging brochures on doors, putting up placards at construction sites, even making cold calls to homes that looked as if they could use work. Now the company logs up to 120 new projects a week into a GIS database, draws a circle with a 0.2-mile radius around each one, and "asks" GeoWizard to pull out the names, addresses, and telephone numbers of the surrounding homeowners.

Before the company starts construction on a new project, high-profile, highly probable prospects in the immediate vicinity receive a soft-sell notice encouraging them to give Archadeck a call if the construction makes too much noise. A second postcard, sent shortly after construction begins, is more suggestive: "We're adding a new deck to 100 Chestnut Street, a couple of doors down. Why not come over and have a look?" After adopting GIS, Archadeck's direct-mail postcard return rate tripled, and the system paid for itself in just a few years.

# Kitten on the Keyboard

**W**hat better (or cheaper) way to market your new product or service than to **tap the thousands of Internet users who belong to special-interest newsgroups**?

Joe Weber, CEO of Narratek, in Brookline, Mass., and his wife, Maria, had developed and patented innovative PC-based software called Smartype, which can reduce a transcriptionist's keystrokes by 70%. The handful of transcriptionists who had purchased the product were experiencing dramatic improvements in productivity. "But," says Weber, "after funding Smartype's development out of our personal assets, we had little money left for marketing. We thought that if we built a better mousetrap, they would come. Not many did." Then Weber discovered an Internet newsgroup for transcriptionists. He provided its subscribers with useful information about Smartype and encouraged them to share their experiences after they had tried it. The result: "The product took off."

However, before you post any promotional message to a newsgroup, be sure that the participants will tolerate solicitations. Many newsgroups are vehemently anti-commercial, and this tactic can backfire if your targeted newsgroup has such a policy. "You shouldn't post something that looks like an ad or a sales pitch," says Weber. "Tact and brevity are essential."

## 13
**IDEA**

# Wanted: Paying Customers

**M**ost companies spend a lot of energy tracking down customers. It helps to have creative ways of finding the right people to whom you should be selling your product or service.

Thomas Beggs, founder of the market-research company Stat One Research, in Atlanta, **regularly combs the "help wanted" ads in the local and national press for prospects**. Indeed, Beggs, who is a part-time M.B.A. student, got his first *Fortune* 500 client by responding to an ad for a paid internship, which he found at his university's placement office. His theory: The ad indicated a need his business might be able to fill. Using the ad as an opening, Beggs followed up with faxes and phone calls until he got an order from the company.

Though the contract was small, Beggs says it was a major milestone for his company, which had sales of about $100,000 in 1997.

# 14
## IDEA

# Filling in the Gaps

**A**ll too often, you get a great sales lead but can't use it because a piece of the information is missing—a zip code, a first name, a full company name, an address. Although Directory Assistance can be useful for hunting down some of this information, it doesn't have all the answers. In such cases, the **World Wide Web's people and business directories** may do the trick. For phone numbers and street addresses, consider www.lookupusa.com, www.four11.com, and www.switchboard.com. To look up e-mail addresses, try www.switchboard.com, www.four11.com, and www.iaf.net. Each site works essentially the same way. If you strike out on one, you may find what you're looking for at another. You can also look up zip codes online at www.usps.gov/ncsc/lookups/lookup_ctystzip.html.

# Taking Stock of the Market

**W**hat does the performance of the stock market have to do with people's craving for chocolate? Not much at first glance, but if you think more about it, the stock market may be a good barometer of consumer confidence and willingness to spend. Knowing when your customers are feeling secure about money allows you to plan your sales strategies.

Adele Ryan Malley, president of Malley's Chocolates, in Cleveland, sells mostly to customers with medium to high household incomes. "The ones who have bigger pocketbooks are usually watching the stock market," she says, "and when that goes up or down, they feel very differently" about discretionary spending. **Watching the same financial indicator that customers are watching** gives Malley's Chocolates the inside knowledge it needs to serve them appropriately—and protect itself from sudden drops in business.

# Our Town

If your company needs a **barometer of America's consumer confidence, try calling the Bureau of Business and Economic Research at Indiana University** (219-237-4288) and ask for information on current economic conditions in Elkhart, Ind.

Why Elkhart? David Pairitz, chief financial officer of Fastec Industrial, a $25-million distributor of industrial fasteners and related products based in the town, says that the community often leads the U.S. economy into and out of recession. One likely reason: Elkhart is a center of recreational-vehicle manufacturing, and RV sales reflect the rising or falling economic confidence of middle-class Americans. Even though Fastec Industrial's sales are national, Pairitz still keeps his eye on business conditions in his neighborhood to stay on top of the market.

# 17
## IDEA

# Make the Past Present

**F**or years, Media Partners Group, a video production company based in Utica, N.Y., sent press releases to area newspapers and trade journals. This tactic generated some news coverage but few new clients. Then, when the group landed a big account, co-owner and marketing director Kim Morrissey decided to **send the same press release to old customers, potential clients, and contacts** she had met at chamber of commerce meetings.

"The immediate feedback was incredible," she says. Former customers called about updating their advertising programs. Casual contacts and potential clients called, too. "They said, 'Hey, I just read that press release. Maybe we should talk about how you can handle our advertising,'" Morrissey reports.

# 18
**IDEA**

## Piggybacking to Market

**T**hey started in a two-bedroom apartment in Woodland Hills, Calif., making phone calls, writing computer code, and working hard to convince their neighbors that they were doing nothing illegal. To attract customers, Elan Susser and Jon V. Ferrara decided they needed to **piggyback onto someone else's selling shoulders**.

Their product—workgroup software designed to help companies share customer information among employees who deal with the same customer—needed the endorsement of a big network user. "I started cold-calling Novell resellers," Ferrara says. "I figured that if I could get a copy into their hands, they would use it, and if they used it, they'd recommend it."

Their shoestring marketing plan turned GoldMine Software into a real player, with 105 employees and revenues of more than $20 million. And from the apartment with two phone lines and a postcard of the beach on the refrigerator, the company has moved to offices overlooking the same beach, near Malibu.

**IDEA 19**

# Don't Toss the Junk Mail

**L**ooking for a big customer to boost your business? Sometimes you can **find sales leads and contact names on product labels or direct-mail pieces**, as Steven Hoeft did.

Struggling along for a few years doing small projects, Hoeft knew he needed a major account to put his direct marketing agency on the map in St. Louis. When a big bank sent him a mailing that he could see needed improvement, Hoeft seized his chance. He called the person who had signed the letter and offered a little advice for free. "I could improve everything—the envelope, the letter, and the offer," Hoeft said. His initial chat was followed by six months of writing proposals and attending meetings— and in the end, S.R. Hoeft Direct landed its largest client. Hoeft's company projects $17.5 million in 1998 revenues.

# 20
**IDEA**

# Look Before You Leap

**E**ven the smallest tweaks in a direct-mail campaign can have significant impact on sales. At Athletic Supply, a 400-employee company in Dallas, vice-president Craig Rosen has made smart mailing his mission. By **analyzing the lifetime value of his customers**, Rosen was better able to evaluate his leads and allocate marketing dollars for his company's award-winning team-apparel catalog. His conclusions:

⮞ *List rental isn't always worth it.* In 1996, Rosen's house list (buyers in his database) yielded three times the net profit per order compared to the average rented list. So Rosen cut back on the number of lists he rents.

⮞ *Big spenders are overrated.* One of the study's big surprises was that "monetary select" wasn't so important. In the past, when Rosen rented lists, he paid considerably more to get people who had histories of spending $50 or more on items from a single catalog. For Athletic Supply, $50-plus buyers weren't more profitable in the long run than a random selection. Rosen stopped paying the premium—and saved $20,000 per year.

⮞ *Print ads generate one-time buyers.* "Someone orders an advertised jersey and never buys again," Rosen says. "Meanwhile, I'm mailing to that person 12 times over the next two years." Not anymore. Rosen has dropped magazine ads because they don't yield long-term customers.

# 21
**IDEA**

## Remodel Your Leads

For five years Paul Eldrenkamp cultivated relationships with architects in hopes of getting referrals for Byggmeister, his home-remodeling business in Newton, Mass. Then sales plummeted during a recession, prompting Eldrenkamp to reexamine his strategy. He discovered that architects generated low-margin jobs because, while clients trusted the architect, they viewed the remodelers as interchangeable and would award business to the lowest bidder. His more profitable referrals came from satisfied customers. From then on, Byggmeister began **selling directly to past customers**, who were less concerned about price and trusted the quality and value of the company's work.

The results were so impressive that Byggmeister no longer advertises in newspapers or the Yellow Pages. Instead, Eldrenkamp spends his marketing dollars where he knows they'll do the most good: servicing warranties for past clients. The new program costs a mere $6,000 a year—less than the amount spent on ads, and the annual check-ins to tighten a cabinet or buff a floor give him a chance to chat up a customer and gather new leads. "Staying in touch with clients, becoming friends, doing things for them, making them happy—it's a lot of fun," says Eldrenkamp. It's also lucrative: Sales now average $1.4 million annually, and profits have increased as well.

**22**

**IDEA**

# Preach to the Converted

**C**hoate Construction, in Marietta, Ga., grew its sales from $17 million to $136 million in five years. By 1997, the company, then nine years old, had sales of $197 million. Indeed, CEO Millard Choate made it his company's mission to be one of the fastest project completion operations in Georgia, and he used that as a selling point. "We show slides of buildings we've done in a short period of time. Normally, that's how we get jobs."

But one potential customer was unimpressed, and Choate was shocked when his proposal was rejected. "They said our company was more powerful than what they wanted. They wanted to go at a sleepier pace." That would have been fine—if only Choate had known. The lesson? **Find out whether your mission statement reflects a prospect's needs and values** before you proclaim it. While corporate mission statements inspire sales representatives onward, they can overwhelm potential sales if you aren't careful.

# 23
**IDEA**

# Swap Shop

**E**xport trading companies, which act as international distributors, can offer a wealth of experience in negotiating the labyrinths of overseas transportation, customs duties, and other regulations. For growing businesses, trading companies can be an inexpensive way to tap foreign markets.

"Different export traders provide different levels of service that have to be negotiated," says Tom Erickson, CEO of The Chromaline Corp., a specialty-chemical company in Duluth, Minn. Once Erickson gained some overseas exposure, he was able to **win synergistic terms with traders**.

Erickson discovered that his company's export trader, H&H Exports, also in Duluth, lacked experience with printing-industry clients. So, he struck a deal. Chromaline gave the export trader a list of hot and cold overseas prospects in exchange for H&H's market research findings. Under the terms of the agreement, Erickson accompanied the export trader on sales calls, while H&H benefited from his introductions to existing clients and familiarity with the industry. H&H Exports handled Chromaline's shipping, documentation, and delivery, and H&H had ultimate control of pricing. Still, Erickson got access to the customer list and numbers. "It was difficult learning how to price," he admits, "so our export trader really helped with that."

When Chromaline started exporting with H&H in 1984, its sales were in the low six figures. The company's sales have since climbed to more than $8.9 million—one-third from overseas—and it has its own corporation in France and a manufacturing facility in India.

# 24
**IDEA**

## Star Gathering

**F**ortunately, expensive focus groups are not the only way to elicit opinions from customers and prospects. You can obtain valuable information by **attending gatherings of hobbyists** who are users of the type of product you sell.

To make sure his company's telescopes meet the needs of customers, Meade Instruments encourages its employees to attend "star parties" held by amateur astronomy enthusiasts and submit their findings to the marketing department. CEO John Diebel says that attending these gatherings gives staffers an opportunity to meet telescope users. They learn what features enthusiasts like and don't like, as well as what changes they'd make to the products. Employees get a kick out of seeing their company's instruments in action, so the outings also help to build loyalty and allow employees who work outside the product-development and marketing departments to contribute in a critical way. Diebel, who started out of his apartment in 1972 with a $2,500 loan from his credit union, has grown the company, based in Irvine, Calif., to more than $60 million in sales.

# 25
### IDEA

## Free Association

**M**any salespeople give thumbs down to ever buying a list of sales leads. Doug Cobb, founder of a subscriber-based newsletter publisher in Louisville, saved his company approximately $10 million in 10 years by sticking to that principle.

During the mid-1980s, software publishers gathered thousands of user names from registration cards. To sell subscriptions to his newsletters, Cobb negotiated deals that allowed his company to use these lists for free. He explained to software marketing departments that subscribing to his newsletter would turn people on the lists into more satisfied customers. Not only did Cobb obtain exclusive access to highly qualified customers, his company operated for years in a market free from competition, as it made exclusive newsletter arrangements with software publishers.

As the software industry has matured, so has its savvy concerning customer lists. Today, getting a look at a list of software buyers generally requires entering a partnership agreement with the publisher. Still, **the best lists in business are free**—company and club directories, customer lists of suppliers related to your industry, and yes, some start-up software-publishing companies are just a few of the places to find great sales leads without great expense.

# Sharpen Your Clauses

If you're in the market for a broker to distribute your product, remember this: Brokers earn most of their money on the buy side of the equation and are notoriously tough negotiators. So to avoid a bad "partnership," listen to what J. Givens Young, the founder and chairman of the Young Pecan Co., the biggest pecan processor in the United States, has learned about **negotiating with a broker**.

*Ask a trade association for the industry's standard commission rate* for brokers. In the pecan business, a broker gets 2%. It's lower for large-volume sales of, say, a half-million pounds, where the broker's contribution to processing the order is smaller. Negotiate a sliding sale commensurate with the broker's work on an account. Is the broker involved in developing the product or simply making a phone call and bidding a price for you?

*Make a list of territories or accounts you want to call on directly.* If a broker isn't interested after seeing your list, it probably means the accounts you kept are a large part of the market, and you don't need a broker.

*Begin talks by offering the broker a fee for introducing your company to customers.* The broker will probably ask for long-term exclusive distribution rights. Walk through, step by step, what the broker's involvement will be in the order process once initial contact is made. If the broker becomes simply a pass-through station for paperwork after the honeymoon is over, make it clear that the relationship is no longer adding value to your company's product. "Most customers want to deal directly and save the commission fee," notes Young, "so don't sign any long-term agreement with a broker."

# 27
## IDEA

# Count on Your Source of Supply

**A** hot tip is better than a cold call, and your suppliers can be excellent sources of warm—or even hot—sales leads. Often they hear about new products and services coming onto the market, someone who's been promoted, or a key contact moving to another company, which signals that the time is ripe for calling on a sought-after account.

Shawn Prior, import manager for Compass Forwarding, a growing international transportation-logistics company based in Jamaica, N.Y., with branch offices in Boston, Atlanta, and Los Angeles, reports that 40% of the new business he generates is the result of **chatting up his suppliers**. "To get referrals from suppliers you have to be an easy customer to do business with," notes Prior. "That means paying your bills on time and not making too many outrageous demands on them. Otherwise, next time they hear about a nice opportunity, they'll tell one of your competitors."

# Divide and Conquer

**B**rooke Barrett, part owner of Manhattan East Suite Hotels, in New York City, resists the temptation simply to assign geographic territories to the sales force, parcel out leads, and get the reps knocking on doors as fast as they can. Instead, her company **gives salespeople specific markets to call on**. "We call on publishers, travel agents, Wall Street, and retail markets. That way our sales representatives are better able to understand their customers' specific needs and peak demand times," she explains. "Some industries get busy around Christmastime, while others require more hotel rooms in the fall."

The system also provides the family-owned hotel chain with a source of market intelligence that drives advertising dollars and promotional packages. "If the company split up Manhattan into geographic slices, we wouldn't be nearly as sensitive to customers' needs," adds Barrett. "Inevitably, bickering over territories and commissions would ensue."

# 29
## IDEA

# Sales Shine at Show Time

Trade shows aren't simply a place to swap business cards and build relationships anymore," says Sam Ganglani, treasurer of Mannix World, a clothing manufacturer and wholesaler in Woburn, Mass. Ganglani, who attends four shows a year, has found that more and more orders are being written there. In his opinion, buyers are being told to refrain from ordering two to three weeks before a show, and companies are allocating money for buying at the show.

"Most people tell me they need to justify attending trade shows to their corporation's accounting department," says Ganglani. Obviously, he thinks **trade-show attendance is a good investment**. To make sure Mannix World's salespeople don't oversell an item, he tallies everyone's orders at day's end, then gives his reps the figures the next morning. Now, instead of pencil and paper, Ganglani takes his inventory program on the road via laptop computer. "The important thing is to keep track," says Ganglani.

# 30
IDEA

# Aim for the Bullseye

**T**o appeal to promising business niches, Michael Kuzma, former vice-president of marketing at Anatomical Chart, in Skokie, Ill., started with **a highly targeted campaign**.

Kuzma mailed a special offer for Anatomical's teaching posters to 9,000 bookstores and followed up with calls to attractive subgroups (such as college bookstores). He limited the trial to what his company could handle without extra hiring by training his top 3 (of 14) customer-service people to work the phones a few hours a day. "A good customer-service person is a telemarketer," Kuzma said.

Their efforts brought in hundreds of qualified leads and landed nearly 100 bookstore accounts. Each store placed an average order of $150 with Anatomical, a 65-employee company that designs and prints anatomical educational aids. Within three months, Kuzma had covered his promotional costs and then some. Even better, Anatomical acquired what are likely to be long-term customers. "Once our display is in the store, it will be there forever, and the stores come back for refills. The lifetime value of the customer is the key," he concluded.

# Customers Can Sell for You

If you need to increase sales, but can't afford a salesperson, what else can you do? Paul G. Lewis, CEO of MC$^2$, a computer network design, installation, and support company in Warren, N.J., decided to **focus his limited selling time on customers who could sell for him**.

Lewis started targeting law and accounting firms, which deal regularly with his potential client base. He figured that if he did a good job for them, they would mention his company to their clients and colleagues. He excelled in his service for his target firms, handed them a stack of his cards when he left, and asked them to recommend MC$^2$.

It didn't take long to see the results. Within two weeks of his first law firm job, Lewis got his first referral. That year, sales grew a whopping 700% over the previous year, and his sales expense was zero. Lewis's revenues have grown to $10 million since 1990.

# 32
### IDEA

## Brewing Brand Management

**N**ews stories about highly successful companies can be a great source of information and inspiration for managers mapping out their company's marketing plans. Problem is, they might miss the follow-up story—if one is done at all. That's why Alan Newman, president and founder of Magic Hat Brewery, in Burlington, Vt., **tracks stories about a handful of companies that sell to the same "psychographic niche"** as he does—companies he admires for their retail savvy and skillful brand management.

"For more than five years I've been following the stories of Benetton, Nike, and Hard Rock Cafe, and recently I added House of Blues to my list," says Newman. "By focusing my attention on a few companies over a longer period of time, I'm able to learn from their mistakes and successes along the way." Newman, who is working hard to build his fledgling brand nationally, reports that the microbrewery sold 15,000 barrels of beer in 1997, its third year of operation.

## 33
**IDEA**

# Quick-and-Dirty Forecasting

**D**ivining the best geographic areas for growing a business can be tough. Lots of CEOs hitch their stars to globe-trotting customers. Some use the results of direct-marketing campaigns.

Russell Inserra, CEO of Orion Construction, in Houston, **studies regional prices** of bulldozers and cranes. Inserra is no economist, but tracking the regional auction prices of heavy equipment has guided the marine contractor past many an economic storm since 1987.

He never bids on contracts, no matter how promising, without also considering the location. To identify up-and-coming states, Inserra compares the prices of the same equipment across the country. The higher the prices, the better the regional economy, he's found. His barometer is on the money about 80% of the time.

When fortunes shift, Orion heads for better pastures. "The country is a big sales territory," Inserra says. "I worked in Florida for two years and pulled out. It wasn't a good market at the time." His eclectic market research helped Orion grow to $31 million by 1997.

# Big Guys Buy More

**S**ometimes, the most efficient route to reaching a customer is not the most direct. For instance, the publisher of *FamilyEducation Today*, a newsletter advising parents on how to get the most out their children's schools, discovered that **piggybacking on large companies** was much more effective than selling direct.

Jonathon Carson, founder of Boston-based FamilyEducation Publishing, discovered that it made more sense to call on CEOs than to launch a massive direct-mail campaign to parents. When he tried a mailing to the *Weekly Reader* list, he got a low 2% response. In contrast, when marketing through a corporation, he found that 10% to 15% of a company's employees typically sign up to receive the newsletter. "We offer a visible benefit that positions a company as family-friendly and concerned with education," says Carson. The newsletter is distributed nationwide to 40 corporations—Bristol Myers-Squibb and Work/Family Directions, among others, purchase it for their interested employees.

So far, some 60,000 parents (and grandparents) of school-age kids receive the complimentary publication eight times a year. The employer's name appears above the logo, and issues can be customized to include, for example, CEO interviews. Companies pay $7 to $18.95 per employee for subscriptions, depending on volume.

Carson knocked on many corporate doors before his big break: The newsletter was handed out at a board meeting of the Business Roundtable, whose members top the *Fortune* 500.

**35**

**IDEA**

# Training for a Chain Reaction

**W**ant to get your product into a big retail chain but having trouble getting an appointment with a buyer and finding out how to handle such a sale? Fear not! **Coaching is available on becoming a vendor to a big chain**.

Entrepreneurs can learn how to win big business by participating in the Support American Made (SAM) program. More than 1,600 small businesses have had their merchandise evaluated by a team of analysts overseen by NaLisa Brown, SAM program manager at Southwest Missouri State University, (501-273-6811). Applicants receive two manuals that recommend corrections for deficiencies, suggest retail outlets suitable for testing products, and offer other relevant entrepreneurial support resources.

Even if a company doesn't make it into, say, Wal-Mart, or finds that the chain is not the perfect outlet for a particular product or line, the exercise isn't futile—all the large chains make similar demands.

# Go for a Broker

**W**hen J. Givens Young started out in the pecan-processing business, he couldn't get in to see the buyers at the big food manufacturers like Kraft, General Foods, Post, and General Mills, so he availed himself of the services of nut brokers who could. Now the Young Pecan Co., in Florence, S.C., is the largest pecan processor and distributor in the world and deals directly with its customers. However, were he starting out from scratch today, company chairman Young says he would still use a broker to gain a toehold in the market.

Young recommends **contacting the buyers for your most important prospects and finding out which broker they prefer** to deal with. Then, open negotiations with brokers by saying, "we are interested in having you introduce us to the major customers for our product," rather than "we are interested in having you represent us." That makes it clear from the outset that your company wants a short-term arrangement—not a long-term, exclusive representation agreement, which can hinder a company's sales and marketing drive over time.

While it's useful to settle on a single broker in a market, Young cautions against signing agreements that last longer than a year. Most companies eventually will want to do business directly and save the 2% brokerage fee. "On very large sales of a million pounds, we wind up talking directly with the buyer to work out product and fulfillment specifications, so we give the broker a fee over a specified time," says Young. "Then it stops."

**37**
IDEA

# Global Exportise

**L**ooking for information that can help you tap foreign markets? When it comes to resources for **developing international trade, start at home—with Web sites and toll-free hotlines**, suggests Spencer Smith, general partner of Business Books Network, a small international publishers' rep based in Dover, N.H. Among the best sources of export expertise are these five, which offer access to market data, industry profiles, trade forecasts, customs regulations, and prospective overseas customers.

&#10070; Trade Information Center, U.S. Department of Commerce (general export assistance); www.ita.doc.gov; 1-800-USA-TRADE.

&#10070; *CIA World Factbook* (statistics and profiles of countries around the world); www.odci.gov/cia/publications.

&#10070; Office of International Trade, U.S. Small Business Administration (Small Business Answer Desk); www.sbaonline.sba.gov; 1-800-U-ASK-SBA.

&#10070; Export Hotline & TradeBank, endorsed by the U.S. Department of Commerce and supported by corporate sponsors (reports on 78 countries; more than 5,000 market reports; industry trends, leads, and contacts; 24-hour fax retrieval); www.exporthotline.com; 1-800-USA-XPORT.

&#10070; Small Business Exporters Association, nonprofit trade and advocacy group representing small and midsize exporters; www.sbea.org/sbea.

# 38
**IDEA**

# Uncle Sam Wants You...to Sign Up for Contracts!

**F**or many businesses, government contracts are like a mirage—so lucrative, yet so far away. But as federal, state, and local businesses privatize certain operations—from janitorial services to food suppliers—there are more and more opportunities for businesses to bid and win contracts. That's especially true for small businesses that can act quickly and curry favor with local politicians.

And now the U.S. government is reaching out to small businesses with a new procurement-related Internet database created by the U.S. Small Business Administration (SBA). Pro-Net, which takes the place of the PASS (Procurement Automated Source System) procurement database, is **a one-stop Web site open to small businesses seeking federal, state, and private contracts**. "Pro-Net gives small companies an edge by providing direct online exposure to contracting officers in charge of the $200-billion federal market," says SBA administrator Aida Alvarez. "Congress, with the support of SBA, recently increased the small-business share of the federal market from 20% to 23%. That's $6 billion more in small-business contracts annually."

Whether or not you want or win a government contract, Pro-Net (http://pro-net.sba.gov) is also a valuable—and free—networking tool that can help small businesses make connections with other small firms to tackle larger, more complex contracts. The Pro-Net database lists more than 165,000 small, disadvantaged, and women-owned businesses, including more than 6,000 firms certified under the SBA's 8(a) business development program. Companies with Internet home pages can link their site to a Pro-Net profile.

# Get Business to Come to You

**A**sk most service providers how they get business and the answer is "referrals" or "word of mouth." Carter Prescott, head of New York-based Carter Communications, which provides high-level writing and speaking services for *Fortune* 500 clients, doesn't even have a listed phone number. "I've never needed one," she says. "It's better to have people call you on their own, rather than soliciting calls anyway. You get a better client that way."

True, but you still have to work to generate referrals. Even your most loyal customers aren't likely to think about generating business for you—they've got their own fish to fry. So try these **sure-fire methods to build your word-of-mouth business**:

1. *Offer incentives for referrals that turn into business.* They can be in the form of discounts on future business, free estimates or samples, or just plain cash. Even a small offer will catch their attention.

2. *Create a referral form and send it to clients or customers* with your invoice for services rendered. If you've done a good job, the time to leverage yourself is upon completion of the project.

3. *Tap your suppliers for leads*, by reminding them that when your business grows, theirs does, too. Spark this exchange by giving leads to your suppliers.

4. *Ask prospects who have turned you down for referrals.* This gives them a graceful exit from a potentially unpleasant task. The only secret, as with any request, is to time it appropriately so that you offer people a natural, unforced opening to help you.

# No Show

**S**alt Marsh Pottery, a company with 25 employees in South Dartmouth, Mass., traditionally sells its specialty hand-painted ceramics to retailers by attending gift-industry shows. In 1997 the company decided to **skip a big trade show** because the prior year's returns of $16,000 hadn't justified the $8,000 it cost Salt Marsh to exhibit.

Instead, co-owners John and Betsy Powel created a one-page sell sheet, complete with four-color photos of Salt Marsh's people and products. They printed it on an ink-jet color printer and sent it to people they had met at previous trade shows who had placed orders. Within one month of the mailing, Salt Marsh had generated the same $16,000 it had the year before.

# Changing Your Swing

**U**ntil you've exhausted all the possible distribution channels, you'll never really know whether you have a best-seller on your hands. When Barney Adams couldn't sell his golf clubs through the major sports chains, he took them to the golf course and began custom-fitting them for clients. Although only 15% of all clubs and accessories are sold through golf course pro shops, Adams Golf's unique "Tight Lies" club suddenly took off. "Within a few months, we went from zero calls to 20 to 30 a week," recalls Adams, founder and CEO of the Plano, Tex., company. How could the company capitalize on the growing popularity of the club before a heavy hitter moved in on the action?

In the fourth quarter of 1995, Mark Gonsalves, vice-president of sales and marketing, convinced Adams to **hire inside salespeople to call retail accounts**. Although many end-users hate to be called at home at night, retailers will take time to listen to a telemarketer's pitch. Since then, sales have grown by 3,500%, and Adams has landed more than 6,000 retail accounts, including many of the same stores he couldn't penetrate years earlier when he called on them in person.

# 42
### IDEA

## Bootstrapping at Showtime

Trade shows can get your product before a target audience, but the cost of exhibiting is often high. Cash-strapped companies can keep the price down by **sharing a booth and exhibiting at less expensive regional shows**.

John Harney, CEO of the $2.5-million tea company Harney & Sons, in Salisbury, Conn., reports that the first five or six years he was in business, he shared a booth at the Fancy Food Show with a friend who was repping canned fish, honey, and a garlic spread. Harney suggests that start-up companies consider regional shows, but a little homework is in order. "Some are dogs," he says. Before you sign on as an exhibitor, check the credentials of the show's management, the history of the show, trends in attendance and sponsor support, and references of major exhibitors.

**43**

IDEA

# The Last Word on a Call

**O**ne thing you don't want to do is go into a sales call and come away with nothing. You can at least get a referral or a lead for another company you may be able to do business with," says Pat Caulfield, cofounder and president of an international customhouse broker and freight forwarder based in Valley Stream, N.Y. Caulfield has grown his company, Evans, Wood & Caulfield, in large part through referrals. Indeed, he makes it a habit to **ask for a lead before leaving a sales call**.

"Recently, I was calling on a customer who didn't have any traffic bound for Italy or England—my company's specialties. However, he referred me to another company in the next town," he says. Caulfield spends three days a week on the road, selling. "Of all the sources of sales leads—newspapers, industry trade lists—personal referrals are by far the best ones for new business, and they don't cost a dime."

# II

"If you can get people to smile
while they give you their money,
you've got it made."

**HAROLD RUTTENBERG**
chairman and CEO, Just for Feet,
Birmingham, Ala.

**IDEA**

# Go Snow City Hall

If you're trying to **sell a product or service to a government agency**—local, state, or federal—be aware that bidding is the rule. That in itself need not put you off. The problem is that the officials who write bid specifications and award contracts take their time and hide behind complicated forms. Vincent Yost, founder of a start-up called Intelligent Devices, in Harleysville, Pa., received the following advice from a panel of seasoned experts about how to sell his company's electronic parking meter to municipalities.

ᘐ *Sell up and down the ladder.* Don't just find the guys who use and service the product—pitch to the councilors and commissioners who may have a stake in boosting revenues from it and can lobby on your behalf.

ᘐ *Use the bidding process to your benefit.* Don't be passive about it. Help the city draft its request for proposals (RFPs), and offer suggestions to help ensure that the published specs include your proprietary features.

ᘐ *Make the bid work double-duty.* Try to turn one sale into several by encouraging municipal "piggybacking." In Ohio, for instance, a properly worded RFP can bring other interested cities under the legal umbrella of a single city's published bid.

ᘐ *Pick the right cities.* If a city council constantly disagrees, bypass that town. Ask the executive director of the division that will use your product what related projects the town has done lately. Has it built any parking garages? Bought any property? If the answer is no, move on. Don't waste your time.

ᘐ *Get another foot in the door.* Hire a high-profile consultant to work on your behalf and become, in effect, an auxiliary salesperson who can recommend your product as part of an action plan.

**45**

**IDEA**

# Show Me Yours, I'll Show You Mine

**B**ob Beck, vice-president of sales at Optio Software, in Duluth, Ga., contends that too many salespeople have "happy ears." They are unwilling to ask the hard "qualifying" questions that indicate whether they should continue to cultivate a relationship with a potential customer. "The prospect is not always right," he says. "That implies a subservient relationship. We present ourselves as consultants whose job it is to find solutions to the problems of our customers. It creates a relationship in which the level of respect is greater at both ends."

To make sure time isn't wasted, Beck promotes **quid pro quo selling**. If a prospect says, "Send me a brochure, and I'll get back to you," he replies, "Okay, I'll send you a brochure if you agree to meet me on Wednesday."

When Beck came on board at Optio Software in 1995, the company had 60 employees and $7 million in revenues. Since then, sales have grown 100%, revenues have jumped to $15 million, and the staff has doubled.

# 46
**IDEA**

## Just Desserts

**Y**ou're inhaling the last string of fettuccine, mopping the last crust of bread through the marinara sauce. Your potential customer sits across from you, frowning. She has finished her meal and is looking as if her mood might be improved by the sight of chocolate. You haven't yet secured the sale. Do you spring for dessert? Of course!

If you were a sales rep for Empower Trainers & Consultants, in Overland Park, Kans., you would have been coached by chief executive Michael May to **order the dessert** (although he might not have told you what kind). According to May, a dessert course gives you more time, and an extra 20 minutes might make a tremendous difference. Dessert also lightens the atmosphere, humanizes the interaction, and is likely to make both you and your prospective client more comfortable. It's hard to take yourself too seriously when you're slurping a caramel sundae—and it just might clinch the sale.

# Who's Who in the Lineup?

**A**s a salesperson, you can't just make people feel important—you have to understand why they are important," says Tom Cottingham, founder of a publisher of Web-related business-to-business newsletters and Web sites based in Louisville. To keep his sales campaigns for NarrowCast Concepts on track, Cottingham makes it a point to **always get a prospect's organization chart**.

"There's usually no policy against handing them out," says Cottingham, who for years had to find his way around the mushrooming Microsoft Corp. while negotiating a variety of agreements for his former employer. For the most part, Cottingham's request for charts has met with little resistance over the years as he sold newsletter-publishing services to major software publishers.

"Most people you ask will be happy to run a copy for you. If you can't get one from an administrative assistant, ask the human resources manager or someone else you've had contact with in the organization," he suggests. If a company refuses to give him a chart, Cottingham draws one himself as he meets people and finds out what their responsibilities are, whom they report to, and what involvement they may have in the project he's pitching. "Selling to any organization," he adds, "requires understanding how everyone contributes to its cohesiveness."

# Present Before You Propose

**D**on't kick off a meeting with a prospective account by distributing your proposal," urges Michael Horgan, founder of JPL Productions, a video production company in Harrisburg, Pa. "If you do, you'll regret it. During the entire meeting, instead of listening to your presentation, they'll be rifling through the proposal and won't hear a word you're saying."

As a former high-school teacher and now a commercial video producer, Horgan is an expert's expert at getting an audience's attention. He always **withholds handouts to prospects until after the sales presentation**. This rule of thumb has helped JPL Productions double its sales since 1991 to more than $4 million.

By giving prospects a sizzling presentation of the material in the proposal, you can ignite the attention of the entire group, overcome objections, and show them your best side. "So often it's not the product that swings a sale but the people making it," adds Horgan.

**49**
**IDEA**

# Warming Up in the Bullpen

**B**elieve it or not, some productivity tools don't cost hundreds of dollars and take AA batteries. Just ask the sales reps at Booklet Binding, in Broadview, Ill. Once, they relied on nothing but low price to sell their company's services in the fiercely competitive printing and binding market. Now they wield powerful pitching spins acquired during a 20-week in-house training program. Here are some of the windups that **help them take control of the selling process**, nearly doubling profit margins and growing sales by more than 30% to nearly $22 million in 1997.

&. *Meeting agendas.* Fax yours before calling on a customer. Scott McParland, a salesman, reports that meetings go much better than they would otherwise, because setting the agenda puts you in charge.

&. *Account profiles.* Have each sales rep develop profiles to find out what percentage of a customer's total business its suppliers are getting. The profile requires salespeople to ask customers what's really important to them and helps them adapt their pitches accordingly.

&. *Calendar log.* Use this type of software to enable salespeople to pre-plan customer orders. "Will we be doing the same saddle-stitching job for you this October?" a rep might ask. It also shows customers that Booklet Binding is thinking about them before the call is placed.

&. *Red Alert Program.* Extend a discount to help attract business during the slow period (in this case, from May through early July). At that time, salespeople offer a discount if printers commit to a job well in advance of the downturn.

# Selling Power on Tap

**E**veryone knows about the power of volume buying, but what about volume selling? Mass sales and distribution channels are also accessible to micromanufacturers and craftspeople, if they join forces with others of their kind.

For example, 40 Oregon microbreweries formed an alliance to educate legislators. They quickly realized that their group had marketing power as well. According to Jerome Chicvara, director of sales and marketing at Full Sail Brewing, which employs 60 people in Hood River, Ore., large, nonguild breweries had begun creating "pseudo-craft brews"—a direct assault on the market served by the Oregon Brewers Guild. So, the guild developed a **common quality-assurance label** that helps differentiate its members from the knockoffs.

Thanks to the power of the group, guild members can also test their products overseas—a complicated undertaking that can overwhelm even the most dedicated loner. "Our product is so high-end that the guy on the other end would never want a full [shipping] container of Full Sail," says Chicvara. "But collectively, we have a portfolio that is very diverse and compelling." Since 1995, Chicvara and seven other guild members have together exported about six shipping containers of beer to Japan, where the appeal of craft brews is just beginning to catch on. They've also wielded their collective clout at home. In 1997 they shared a booth and expenses at a Chicago trade show, where Chicvara landed a distribution deal with a 90-store chain in Indiana—not for himself but for four of his competitors.

51
**IDEA**

# Cooperative Competition

Increasing competitive pressures from abroad, plus a trend by big companies to consolidate supplier bases, have led many small companies that would normally compete to **form strategic partnerships to win business**. Banded together, they can bid on contracts that require more expertise than each can provide individually. And often, two companies that appear to be direct competitors really have specialties that are complementary.

Since 1993, the revenues of Anson Machine and Manufacturing, which designs and manufactures machinery in Louisville, have skyrocketed from $3 million to $80 million in revenues, thanks to John R. Anson's aggressive pursuit of major contracts that each require input from a number of small companies like his own. Anson began by bidding on a $15-million General Electric contract that required cooperating with two of his biggest competitors. In 1998, Anson will get $60 million worth of work from GE. He serves as the trio's contact person and coordinates the work. Now he works with more than a dozen different companies on large contracts. If he hadn't gone co-op, Anson figures his expansion costs would have run $15 million more than the $40 million he's invested over the past five years.

## Sharing Their Toys

**W**hen Judy Cockerton, co-owner of two Massachusetts toy stores (No Kidding!, in Brookline and Mattapoisett), runs out of stock, she goes to any lengths to replace it—even calling a competitor. She knows that her customers will remain loyal if she can produce the toy they're looking for, when they're looking for it.

Her company has **formed a marketing alliance with other independent retailers** in the area to battle a common enemy: big toy chains. Now, when Cockerton explains her shortage to one of her five partners, the other toy store takes the order over the phone at no extra charge. Though careful not to discuss pricing to avoid violating antitrust laws, the group cohosts promotional parties, holds joint raffles, offers a collective frequent-buyer card, and obtains bulk discounts. "When you're competing with all the specialty franchises and Toys 'R' Us, this seems to be the smartest way to do it," says Cockerton, who employs more than 20 staffers.

# He's No Slouch

**W**hen Bob Black was a high-school biology teacher, he made it a point to look to his students for clues to the effectiveness of his performance. Although Black's teaching days are long past, he still depends on this skill to guide him through sales appointments with prospective customers of his company, Super Wash, in Morrison, Ill.

As he pitches car-wash installations, Black **pays close attention to prospects' body language**. "Are they sitting on the edge of the couch, eager to hear what I say next? The ones that aren't with me will check the clock, fidget, ask questions right away. I know that I've turned the light on in their heads when they sit back in the couch and relax," says Black. When he sees signs that a prospect trusts him, he delivers the confidential financial information that he wouldn't want to fall into a competitor's hands, then goes in for the close. Black's results? Super Wash boasts $32 million in annual revenues—and he's its only sales representative.

# 54
**IDEA**

## Look on the Laptop

**W**hat do you do when a prospect doesn't know which of your products or services to order? What if he asks about your potential production schedules or who would be working on the project? At Sealund Associates, a $2-million publisher of technical manuals based in Clearwater, Fla., sales reps can delve into a **laptop computer database for answers to detailed questions**—information even an armload of project samples can't demonstrate, especially if you're in the middle of a meeting.

"We want each team member working on a project to upload raw notes of telephone conversations with clients and summaries of their work—typos and all—to the database within 24 hours," says founder Barbara Sealund. With the price of computer memory constantly dropping and the quality of search tools so high, spelling and grammar are secondary to keeping the database information-rich and current. The company even sends project updates via e-mail to team members working in remote locations. When sales representatives search the database for past customers that had the same needs as a current prospect, the reps find out what tools—such as video training or a handout—helped other customers meet the same goals. "Using the database on a laptop makes prospects sit up and take us seriously," says Sealund.

**55**

**IDEA**

# Culture Vulture

**G**ood salespeople don't waste time looking out the window when in a prospect's office, they **read the walls and bookcases for clues to break the ice**. "You need to get into the inner office before you can begin to state your message," explains Chuck Piola, president of NCO Financial Systems, a $125-million Pennsylvania collections agency.

Piola, an *Inc.* 500 alumnus, once called on a dentist who had a photograph of Mozart's house on his waiting-room wall. "I bet you no salesman had ever asked him about that picture. I told him I was there for the Mozart Festival, and he asked me into his office. None of my salespeople had ever gotten in to see him." Recently, Piola spied a hardcover copy of Tom Clancy's latest book on someone's desk. "The first thing I said was, 'That's the best book he ever wrote,' and the guy totally opened up to me."

To break down barriers and find common ground with a prospect, keep up with pop culture by reading mass-circulation magazines like *People*, best-selling fiction, and the local newspaper. Follow popular sports and pastimes like antiquing and golf. These leisure activities keep you in touch, not only with the world, but with your prospects as well.

# 56
**IDEA**

## High-Caliber Bullets

**D**esign Basics, a home-plan publisher, risks losing sales to its competitors because the home builders who sell its products don't represent Design Basics exclusively. To avert ineffective secondhand sales pitches, Design Basics **writes and delivers the script for independent sales reps**.

Each page of the home-plan summary that a builder-rep shows a prospective home buyer comes complete with a detailed, bulleted list of the design's highlights. For instance, while a competitor's plan might simply state that a house is "sunny," a Design Basics summary specifies "double doors in southern exposure provide ample light."

"We spell out the features builders take for granted, so they don't have to fish for words," explains Linda Reimer, president of the $4-million firm based in Omaha. And when home buyers are left to look over a stack of plans, Design Basics sales copy demystifies the details. According to a survey of 300 builders, 90% of them liked the sales copy with its bulleted highlights.

In addition to providing a ready-made sales pitch, Design Basics publishes illustrations that maintain clarity and crispness when faxed. If reps require sales materials on the spot or need to fax illustrations to a prospect, Design Basics plans received by fax can compete with other companies' slick presentations that the prospect might already have.

# 57
**IDEA**

# Tools of the Trade

**S**trategies for **maximizing the payoff you get from trade shows** can be as simple as sending out follow-up faxes to leads and can increase returns exponentially. Look at the following examples.

Frank Candy, president of the American Speakers Bureau, in Orlando, writes about 200 personal invitations to prospects asking them to visit his booth. The invitations, which look like greeting cards, cost the company less than $1 apiece. The first time he tried it, 37 prospects showed up, boosting show-generated sales by more than 300% over those from the previous year's show. "It was by far the most effective tool I've found in 15 years and at hundreds of shows," says Candy.

To focus sales pitches better, the sales staff of Insight Imaging Systems, a San Carlos, Calif., manufacturer of dental technology products that is now part of New Image Industries, drew up a list of questions to ask prospects at the booth. Before one show, the sales team attended a role-playing seminar on getting information from potential customers without turning them off. The result? The $20-million company wrote $1 million in trade-show orders, up from $600,000 the preceding year.

I/O Data Systems, a computer reseller in Bay Village, Ohio, converts leads into paying customers by sending booth visitors a monthly broadcast fax of sale prices. The $2-million company spends about $10,000 a year on follow-up faxes and phone calls. It usually breaks even on a show within three months. "The rest of the year brings in about $30,000 in profits," says CEO Tom Tont.

**58
IDEA**

# Reach for the Stars

**C**an your sales force explain to prospects how much power your gizmo has and how it works? Or do they have to hunt in the manuals to find obscure facts and figures too complex to memorize? In either case, the answer to technical questions may fail to communicate to customers the true benefits of a product. "People buy an experience, not a product," says John Diebel, founder, chairman, and CEO of Meade Instruments, a telescope manufacturer.

Diebel has been teaching people **how to answer innocent but deadly questions** about his telescopes for more than 30 years. "Nine times out of 10, when people walk into a store, they ask how much magnification power a telescope has, rather than how it performs," he says. He advises store clerks to delay questions about power until they discuss the product's advantages and the importance of the telescope's aperture. "We suggest saying, 'I'll be glad to answer your question about power, but let me assure you that it's not that important. Let me tell you what you'll be able to see with each of the telescopes.'" Then the salesclerk can easily explain how you'll see Saturn with the low-end model, but for an extra $100 you can see Saturn's rings, and if a customer splurges for the high-end instrument, the major divisions in Saturn's rings are visible. After that, if a customer is still interested in power questions, it's easier to focus on a specific model and the buyer's budgetary needs. This tactic has helped the company, located in Irvine, Calif., propel sales to more than $60 million.

## 59
### IDEA

# Ally with Inside Assistants

**H**aving a tough time getting in to see a decision maker? Maybe you aren't talking to the right people. According to Tom Cottingham, founder of NarrowCast Concepts, in Louisville, and a veteran sales representative, **a prospect's administrative assistant can be a sales rep's best ally**. "Administrative assistants are some of the most important people I call on," he says. "They may not control the checkbook in a company, but they control another commodity just as important: company time."

Some aggressive salespeople squander great leads because they don't introduce themselves properly—offending the gatekeeper—and then can't get appointments. Others give as little information as possible to people who surround key decision makers. Cottingham cultivates administrative assistants by letting them know his agenda. By confiding in them, he often gains their trust and is able to line up an appointment with their bosses. "They'll say, 'Well, he's really busy but he's got a half hour on Tuesday at 1:30, so if you show up then he may be able to see you.' Sometimes these executives can see me, and sometimes they can't. If they can't, then I just thank the assistant for trying and try to find another time to try again."

# They Can't Say No

One of the best ways to ask for an order is to **ask questions that can't be answered in the negative**. Take the strategy Kevin Harper uses to cultivate customers for his Bristol, Vt., company, Autumn Harp, which designs and manufactures skin care products for cosmetics companies and under its own brand.

"We don't ask if we can make and package lip balm for them," says Harper. Instead, his team meets with a prospect's design department and unveils a prototype tailored to its needs and brand identity. Then Autumn Harp tweaks the sample with the designers. "At this point," explains Harper, "the prospect has confided in us. It knows we are a good fit with its line and gives us the informal nod. Then we'll get the formula just right and present the sample again."

If it meets with approval, Harper offers to proceed with testing. If the prospect agrees, he says, "Before we go any deeper into the research and development of this project, we need to discuss how much of the product you think you can sell and how committed you are to doing business with us. If we can settle on a contract, then we can fold the testing fees into the overall price of the product. Otherwise, we'll need a fee to cover the costs of the three-month trial tests." Then Harper goes for the close and asks, "How do you want to handle it?"

# Selling the Superstores

**G**iant retail chains can put even tiny manufacturers in the national limelight overnight. But getting onto the giants' shelves isn't easy, and staying there is harder still. Here are some **tips for getting your foot in the door at superstores**:

&> *Get contacts.* Identify the right contact at headquarters, but don't go above the buyer's head.

&> *Go to trade shows.* These are excellent places to meet buyers you've been trying to contact. "I like to see people [there] we'd otherwise never be exposed to," says Target buyer Teri Kohler.

&> *Be knowledgeable and opportunistic.* Know the competition and the consumer. Be ready with promotional ideas.

&> *Get a second order.* An initial order is a test, but initial orders don't really count. "Product innovation and packaging got us in the door," says John Stone, president of Opus, a Bellingham, Mass., manufacturer of bird feeders. "What you do beyond that is what keeps you in."

A 1998 study of sales practices found that customers increasingly value direct contact with top brass. Of 1,063 decision makers surveyed, 22% said business owners or executives play an important role in the purchasing process—up from 8% four years earlier.

**H.R. CHALLY GROUP**
Dayton, Ohio

# Good Humor for Cold Calls

**P**atty Glass, the owner of a $600,000 art consultancy in Cincinnati, finds she gets good results on the phone by coming clean right away. Here's one variation of her approach:

"Hi, this is Patty Glass with The Art Company, and this is a cold call. I bet you get a million of these. Fasten your seat belt—here's another one."

**After a humorous start, she gets to the point quickly** and doesn't waste the prospect's time. She's discovering that her lighthearted approach can work for others too: She recently shared it with her latest hire. The new salesperson, Glass reports, soon generated $11,800 in sales from about 55 names on a list that the rest of the staff considered "dead."

**63**
**IDEA**

# Slide into Home Base

**W**hen Howard Getson isn't selling his company's sales-automation software, he can be found pitching to private investors—widely acknowledged as some of the toughest customers on the planet. By the end of the first quarter of 1998, Getson had hauled in more than $10 million for IntellAgent Control, in Dallas. One of his favorite selling tools is **a slide show** because it gives prospects confidence in his abilities. "I do so much preparation that it looks effortless," he says. "People remember things with a lot more depth and clarity if you combine visuals and text."

Anyone with an appropriate slide show, Getson also contends, will be perceived as better prepared. In addition, the slides enable him to control the order and timing of the presentation—and step around questions that could trip him. "Hey, you know, I've got something about that a couple of slides ahead," he'll respond to an unwelcome inquiry. "But I want to make a couple of other points first."

Of course, it only works if prospects agree to watch the slide show, which they do because Getson gives them a choice—or seems to. If he senses resistance, he simply waits until the right moment to mention that he's prepared a few slides. Once the curtain rises, the graphics flow naturally with his explanations. When Getson talks about what most salespeople want from automation software, a proposal slides out of a computer, followed by a price list. The visuals and handouts, he says, "make me seem smart, practical, and grounded."

64
**IDEA**

# Fast, Cheap, and in Control

Even before the Internet and e-mail became powerful business selling tools, Dennis Gillings's employees and managers never found it difficult to picture what he was talking about on the phone. The CEO of Quintiles Transnational, in Durham, N.C., would address groups over the speakerphone while his employees in another Quintiles office—perhaps on a different continent—watched an accompanying slide show. This solution cost a fraction of what a slick videoconference would cost and was just as effective.

For companies doing business in remote locations or across time zones, **combining slides and speakerphone** can help save loads of money and clear up any confusion about a product, process, or price quote. Since most companies have slide projectors, sending some slides in advance and setting a specific time for the telephone call is a great way to get employees and customers to make a serious commitment to teleconferences.

Quintiles, a full-service contract pharmaceutical organization, has grown rapidly while remaining consistently profitable. Much of the growth has come from international markets. The company opened its first overseas location in 1987; in 1998 it has offices in 28 countries. Fifty-five percent of its business is now done outside the United States.

**65**

IDEA

# Short and Sweet

**G**ot a minute? In Matt Hession's experience, just about everyone does. And besides, once people saw Hession take off his watch, they couldn't wait to take in his **60-second sales pitch**. "They thought it was fascinating," says the former president of Key Medical Supply. "They would say to themselves, 'Hey, the entertainment just walked in.'"

Hession could see that pharmacists were "busy, busy people," with doctors and patients always phoning and customers perpetually lined up for prescriptions. He concluded that to interest them in a partnership aimed at selling or leasing medical equipment, such as wheelchairs and oxygen concentrators, he'd need a catchy sales presentation that took up little of their time but still laid to rest their biggest fears. "If I walked in looking like a salesman," says Hession, "the pharmacist wouldn't want to buy anything or talk to me. I nullified that feeling right off the bat. The pharmacist would think, 'it's only a minute, and it doesn't cost anything.' I wasn't threatening anymore."

Customers smiled; they wanted to hear what Hession had to say. He took off his watch to show that he was serious and told them when the minute was up, because he wanted them to know that he meant what he said. Pharmacists were impressed that he managed to pull it off.

When Hession called the next week, he simply said, "This is Matt. I did the one-minute presentation. Have you had a chance to read over the contract I left with you?" They always remembered him. In one year, Key Medical, located in Thibodaux, La., blanketed the state, signed on 200 pharmacists, and recorded sales of $3 million.

66
**IDEA**

# Getting to Yes, After All

I don't think of myself as a salesperson," says Kim Whittaker. But the president of Baby Faire, a product, services, and information expo for prospective parents, is just that. She persuaded the late, great Dr. Benjamin Spock to headline her first consumer show, in Boston—on his 90th birthday. And she's recruited such sponsors as John Hancock, Prudential Insurance, Toys 'R' Us, Gerber Products, and drugstore chain CVS.

"Most of my sponsors and exhibitors said no before they said yes. **Usually, no is a request for more information**," Whittaker notes. She received a rejection letter from CVS, but she didn't give up. A second round of sleuthing revealed that the drugstore chain had produced its own consumer show, with mixed results. A follow-up letter, which compared the setup of CVS's show to Baby Faire's, won her a face-to-face meeting with CVS executives and, two weeks after that, a major sponsor.

Generally, people are willing to talk if you call and say you'd like to discuss what went into their decision. But, Whittaker adds, "you have to hear what they're saying. Usually, I uncover a misconception about Baby Faire." Whittaker, whose five shows drew 75,000 attendees in 1997, has learned how hard to push and when to get off the phone. She concludes, "The door is never closed if you believe the opportunity still exists." In eight years of persuading people to reconsider, Whittaker, based in Winchester, Mass., has built a thriving business.

# 67
**IDEA**

# A Little Help from Your Friends

It takes time and effort to get customer references, but many companies don't use their customer lists to solicit references effectively. This is despite the fact that references can be one of your best sales tools. Here are some **pointers for helping customers "sell" for you**:

⮞ *Make it easy for prospects to check on you.* Business Interiors, a fast-growing office-furniture dealer in Irving, Tex., lists in its brochure the addresses and phone numbers of 15 to 20 references.

⮞ *Exceed expectations.* Lots of companies hand out a glossy sheet of paper listing the names of a dozen or so customer references. Gunn-Mowery Insurance Group, an $11-million insurance brokerage in Lemoyne, Pa., gives prospects a longer list of its top 50 clients, including the most recognizable names. "When we were unknown, it helped legitimize the company," says president Greg Gunn.

⮞ *Thank references.* At Indy Lube, customers who send friends to the $10-million Indianapolis-based quick-lube chain get a $10 certificate toward their next oil change. Customers fill out a referral card and give it to a friend, and the friend uses the card to get $5 off his or her first oil change. When Indy Lube runs a contest among its 29 locations for most referrals in a month, CEO Jim Yates says he redeems as many as 50 cards a store.

# 68
## IDEA

# K.I.S.S. at Work

**W**hen mounting competition threatened C.A. Short Co.'s growth, president and CEO Charles Davis figured that the fastest way to expand sales for the company, which manages recognition award programs for employers, was to bring in an army of sales reps to reach beyond its market at the time—the few states close to the company's Shelby, N.C., headquarters. But only a handful of the 30 new reps he recruited had ever sold recognition programs, so Davis knew he'd have to systematize the selling process to keep track of customers and provide support for his reps.

He developed a **new selling process with a one-page Recognition Needs Analysis** (RNA) as its cornerstone. The RNA's questions lead the reps through their initial contact with prospects—prompting them to ask about problems that recognition programs might address, programs already in place, and budgetary outlines. The reps then transmit the RNAs to headquarters via mail, fax, e-mail, or the company's Web site. Then the home office generates a sales proposal within five days.

"The RNA frees the salesperson to sell," says Davis. It cuts sales time in half because there's less of an administrative burden. And knowing how quickly the home office will have the proposals ready, reps can set up callback appointments during their first call.

Following the launch of the new program (and the purchases of two companies), sales grew from $1.3 million to $44 million in four years.

**69**
**IDEA**

# Senses and Sensibility

**W**hen competition for a new account is stiff, your product's high quality can get drowned out by a persuasive sales pitch from a competitor's magnetic salesperson. That's why Michael Horgan, founder of JPL Productions, a video-production company based in Harrisburg, Pa., one-ups the competition during a bid process. JPL produces actual video-clip samples for a prospect, instead of storyboards and scripts as most video production companies do.

"You need to push all the buttons possible to ignite a customer's imagination and prove that your company is the best one to do the work," says Horgan, who tries to **appeal to all five ways people learn: written, verbal, visual, kinetic, and experiential**. "Usually my vision is more elaborate and expensive than what the customer has in mind. By pulling all these levers, I make sure I drive my message home." Horgan says the technique has helped him double his company's annual sales since 1991 to more than $4 million.

# 70
## IDEA

# Dealing with Your Dealers

**M**ost dealers are set up for failure," says Ed Gannon, former director of HBO & Company's CyCare Business Group, in Dubuque, Iowa. How so? Companies often expect their independent dealers to shoulder the job of creating new-product demand.

Before introducing SpectraMed, a $5,000 software program used to manage small medical practices, Gannon **asked his dealers what they wanted** from CyCare. "To a person, they said, 'If you focus on the national campaign, we'll take care of regional activities,'" he relates.

The 160 dealers agreed to give up some margin to help fund a national advertising campaign. Gannon tested potential ads on doctors and surveyed two years' worth of magazines before selecting nine journals. The ads included an 800 number to call for a free video—a project Gannon funded by trading in an unprofitable $10,000 trade-show booth.

All leads from the national ads were passed on to the dealers. In the first four months, they sold nearly 500 units—giving CyCare its best year ever.

# 71
**IDEA**

# The Winning Team

**W**hen Ann Machado uses **team selling to win the big accounts**, she really means *team*. The CEO of $15-million Creative Staffing, a temporary-services firm in Miami, fields a lineup that includes Machado, her chief financial officer, her sales director, the sales rep, the operations manager, and the person who would service the account.

"When you explain what each person does, it gives you more credibility," says Machado. Customers concur. "It's nice to have access to all the players. You know who's going to carry out the service," says one.

Machado, who spends 10% of her time on team sales, says the tactic lowers selling costs. Previously it could take six months to close a major deal; now it takes as little as five weeks because the team gathers more and better information, she says. While the CEO tackles issues such as workers' comp, the sales director may assess the fit between the two companies.

One drawback: The limited time to establish a rapport. In a 45-minute meeting, you can overwhelm the prospect, Machado warns. However, the team usually leaves with a small order that day. Team selling has netted Creative Staffing one new contract worth $2.5 million. And the team saved two $1-million contracts that were under attack by a competitor.

# Cool Juice, Hot Sales

**B**eing unable to get your bottled drinks onto supermarket shelves may point you to more original outlets. Urban Juice & Soda, in Vancouver, B.C., can't afford to stock its brands in supermarkets because of prohibitive slotting fees. "I can't play that game right now," says founder and CEO Peter van Stolk. "Even if I could pay for the space, I'd have to create the pull, and that takes marketing dollars." So, until he can afford to sell Jones Soda and Wazu bottled water in supermarkets, van Stolk **targets nontraditional venues**: tattoo parlors, snowboard shops, and navel-piercing establishments, as well as bagel shops, cappuccino bars, and Chinese restaurants—"anywhere Coke and Pepsi won't go or can't go."

Without competing in big, traditional markets, van Stolk has managed to grow his company from $3 million in 1995 sales to a projected $21 million in 1998. And he has established his product on the hip, Gen-X circuit—a very thirsty crowd with a future.

## 73
### IDEA

# Nonprofit for Profit

**W**hen drastic changes in the marketplace create big problems for your company, you may find solutions in your own backyard— if you're willing to work *with* the competition rather than against it. **Contact other companies operating in your niche within the region, join forces, and become the industry's nerve center**, much like Wichita became known as the hub of the aviation industry.

When military cutbacks hit the fiber-optics industry, Bill Hanley, CEO of $34-million Galileo Corp., in Sturbridge, Mass., persuaded five competitors to make the pie bigger by marketing themselves together. His proposal: promote the Sturbridge area as home to a fiber-optics brain trust. The group—now comprised of 12 companies—formed a separate, nonprofit entity called the Center for Advanced Fiber Optic Applications, which markets the combined capabilities of its member companies. Hanley reports that there are a dozen cooperative projects in the works and that member companies are independently selling smaller, joint projects outside the center.

# Coalition in the Cards

**A**s a shoestring company in the shadow of a giant, how can you hold your ground? Alan and Natalia Wolan, cofounders of Five Fingers, a New York City company that sells advertising on postcards, found strength in numbers. Their strategy: **Join forces with other small companies outside your territory**.

The Wolans found several competitors in the same cash-poor position as their company. In Los Angeles, Pik:nik's founder, Annett Sell, was lugging postcards around the city herself. Similar competitors in Chicago and Florida shared a sense of urgency as competitor Max Racks, a company whose war chest they estimated to be close to $1.5 million, poised itself to march through as many major metropolitan areas as possible.

At a summit meeting in 1995, the small companies realized it would be in everyone's best interest to work together and decided to link up. That enabled them to sell national distribution to big accounts such as the Gap, Tanqueray, and Hanes. The coalition, later named GoCard, now has seven companies in 14 cities.

# Associated Press

**A**s a financial planner and investment adviser, Betty Hedrick knows the value of numbers. By cross-promoting The Hedrick Co., her $600,000 business, with six other small business-to-business service providers, Hedrick gains a community of helpful colleagues and access to new prospects. The cooperative arrangement also enhances her company's image and boosts sales.

The seven companies **jointly produce a quarterly newsletter and mail it to all their clients**. While none of them could do it alone, working together keeps the burden manageable and costs affordable. Plus, the shared newsletter "expands the types of expertise available to our clients," says Hedrick, who is based in Mercer Island, Wash. Every company involved gets introduced to the others' clients, expanding everyone's base of potential customers—while offering a wider range of services to the ones they already have.

76
**IDEA**

# An Introduction to Royalty

Instead of building your own sales force to market and sell your company's proprietary product, it may make sense to **structure a royalty arrangement with a large company that already controls a dominant position in the market you want to reach**. Ian Kibblewhite wasted a year casting about for partners before he hooked up with a "matchmaker," Technology Management and Funding (TMF), in Princeton, N.J., which pairs promising start-ups with big corporations.

Kibblewhite's company, Ultrafast, possessed proprietary technology for a bolt tightener and a coating to make the fastener work. TMF arranged for him to license his bolt-tightener technology to two large corporations, reserving the right to manufacture and sell the company's bolt coating himself. The price of using such a matchmaking service can be steep: Kibblewhite gave TMF 20% of the equity in Ultrafast. Still, he felt the investment was worth it: In return for coexclusive rights to produce the bolt fasteners, two European manufacturers forked over more than $1 million each and pledged future royalties of 5%—plus, Ultrafast could look forward to future sales of the coating.

# Paying Homage to Royalty

**Y**ou are convinced that your new invention is destined to be the bedrock of a new company. If so, ask yourself these questions: Do I want to own 60% of a company that has to clear all the market hurdles from scratch? Or would I be better off, for example, with a 10% royalty on the top line of a licensed product that is being pushed through the distribution channel by an entrenched competitor?

"Most new ventures are products, not companies," asserts Bill Sahlman, a Harvard Business School professor. "Unfortunately, most entrepreneurs are blinded by their obsession with control."

Sahlman suggests that the quickest and most lucrative route to success may be to **farm out the sales and marketing responsibilities to another company** that already has coveted contacts with targeted customers. Your product still gets sold—and you still realize a profit.

# 78
**IDEA**

## Bottoms Up!

**M**aking a major sale is a process of nurturing relationships, egos, and interest within an organization while pushing your own company's agenda. "Nobody likes carrying someone else's water," says Tom Cottingham, who honed his selling skills for the last 15 years negotiating complicated multimillion-dollar joint venture agreements. "It's got to be the middle manager's idea that's blessed from above."

Cottingham, who started his own newsletter-publishing venture, NarrowCast Concepts, in 1997, prefers the **top-bottom-top approach to sales**. "You meet a senior person at a conference and explain your plan. You see eyes sparkle. To me, that means take the sale to the next step. So, then you go to a middle manager and casually mention that the senior manager liked the idea." According to Cottingham, the worst thing a sales rep can do at this juncture is get the senior-level person to issue a memo. Instead, Cottingham recommends brainstorming with the middle manager on the project and allowing him or her to have highly visible input. That may mean verifying the company's need and enlisting the middle manager to help sell the concept within the organization. Then the middle manager can present the fleshed-out proposal to the senior manager for approval.

# We Wanna Hold Your Hand

For Ned Lamont, the first sale was plain luck, and the next sale was plain hell. When the CEO of Campus TeleVideo, based in Greenwich, Conn., first started promoting his cable television systems to universities, the academics snubbed him. When direct mail and trade shows also failed to convert leads, Lamont **focused on the objections of customers and prospects and fine-tuned his sales pitch**. Customers, he says, "have written our whole strategic plan for us." A decade later, Lamont has made sales to 85 universities, to the tune of $10 million in 1997, using these strategies.

❧ *Walk customers through every stage of a long-term project.* Campus TeleVideo, which lays cable, installs satellite dishes, and arranges for educational programming, conducts walk-through tours for a range of campus decision makers—from dorm directors to the director of telecommunications, and from the student-body president to the university president. Tours are held before the sale, during the installation, and at the project's completion, giving everyone a chance to voice concerns along the way.

❧ *Invite prospects to meet customers.* Lamont used that tactic to help increase his business more than threefold in five years. During an installation at Kent State, for example, Campus TeleVideo asked representatives from five Ohio-area schools to drop in; they did, with lots of questions. Not long after, Lamont was invited to bid on three Ohio college contracts, and he won the only one awarded.

❧ *Host informal focus groups.* Once a year Campus TeleVideo invites customers and prospects to an all-day focus group at which it introduces new products, and participants swap ideas about programming.

# III

"No sale is a good sale unless it's
a good value for the customer."

**STANLEY MARCUS**
chairman emeritus, Neiman Marcus,
Dallas

**IDEA**

# Better Than Pulling Teeth

**M**arketing a new product can seem like tilting at windmills—especially when you're a small start-up and the competition consists of such giants as Bausch & Lomb, Braun, and Teledyne. Such was the challenge faced by Optiva, a Bellevue, Wash., maker of the Sonicare toothbrush, a device that uses sound waves traveling through fluid to erode the plaque off teeth.

David Giuliani, one of Optiva's founders, lent authority to his company's claims for its product, first by **commissioning a study demonstrating its effectiveness, then asking experts to "invest" in the product**.

Armed with a report that showed use of the Sonicare toothbrush could lead to a reduction in bacteria below the gumline, the Optiva crew set up a tiny booth at a dental convention in Orlando. Unlike its competitors, the company didn't give the product away to dentists but charged them a small fee for it, which was only a fraction of the $129 retail price. This made the relationship between the company and the dentists one of mutual respect, rather than one doing favors for the other. "I thought the dentist should feel invested in the product," says Giuliani. "Plus, it gave us a little money."

The company's strategy paid off: Optiva holds 40% of the market for electric toothbrushes sold directly from dental practices, and it ranked No. 1 on the 1997 *Inc.* 500 list of the fastest-growing private companies in the United States.

**81**

**IDEA**

# Please Screen Our References

**R**ather than simply list references for a prospect to call, Lee Kirkwood **makes his proposal stand out from others by including a video of customer testimonials**. Kirkwood is the owner and CEO of United Mail, a Louisville company that sells direct-mail and mailroom-management services.

In the five-minute video, customers from *Fortune* 500 companies tell why they chose United Mail, what services it provides, and other positive comments about working with the company. "It's more than print communication. Through the video testimonials, our services come alive for prospects, and it drives home to them that even though we may not be a brand name, big-name companies avail themselves of our services," says Kirkwood, whose "unknown" company grew to $25 million in 1997 and competes against the giants for accounts.

# Slam Dunk into the Big Leagues

The American Basketball League's (ABL's) line of business—professional women's basketball—isn't quite your standard Silicon Valley fare, but CEO Gary Cavalli insists he comes "from the Silicon Valley mentality that business is war." Cavalli's stance is probably appropriate because the ABL needs every play in the book to avoid getting stuffed by its competitor, the Women's National Basketball Association (WNBA), which is owned by the NBA. How does the ABL—a scrappy upstart based in Palo Alto, Calif.—go about taking on a giant such as the WNBA?

"Not having the big war chest," says Cavalli, "we **take the product to the consumer and maintain a one-brand focus**." His marketing strategy follows the "hit 'em where they ain't" sports theory. You'll find ABL players stumping for their employer at malls and church leagues where they have exclusive audiences. And ABL contracts, which average $70,000, include noncompete clauses. "If your stars are playing in both leagues," reasons Cavalli, "their brand value is diluted."

**83**
**IDEA**

# Outstanding in the Field

You wouldn't want your customers to watch your employee training sessions, would you? Well, maybe you should! Ruppert Landscape, based in Ashton, Md., has **customers judge trainees on their latest efforts at a Field Day** for all its workers. The event is held in a public location earmarked for free landscaping. As members of panels, the customers award points for everything from truck cleanliness to laying sod.

This charitable demonstration allows employees to understand what customer expectations are and provides an entertaining setting for salespeople and customers to mingle and talk shop. It also shows customers how seriously Ruppert takes its business. In an industry where well-trained employees are the exception rather than the rule, Field Day is a great way to showcase the company's continuously improving teams. Best of all, a public space becomes more beautiful in the process.

Ruppert Landscape held its first Field Day in 1981, when the company's revenues were less than $1 million. Sixteen years later, 700 employees worked on the grounds of 24 Washington, D.C., public schools, where several superintendents served as judges. As a result of the exposure, Ruppert—making annual sales of approximately $40 million in 1997—was asked to bid on several school-related projects.

# 84
**IDEA**

# Patience Makes Perfect

**W**hen Norm Brodsky went into a large accounting firm in New York City to pitch CitiStorage, his archive-retrieval business, he knew he'd need to offer more than good prices to woo the customer away from its current storage company. "I have to tell you," said the partner with whom Brodsky met, "I've been doing business with these people for a very long time, and I like them." No amount of talking—or price-cutting—was going to win over this customer.

So Brodsky asked to spend some time in the firm's records room. He told the partner, "Records management is my business. I can **offer some suggestions on how to improve your system and generate substantial savings**." Two hours later, Brodsky reported the inefficiencies he had found. "There were too many boxes on the premises," he says. "The firm was constantly having to send some back to make room for new ones. As a result, it wound up ordering—and paying for—five deliveries a week, instead of only one." Brodsky also offered to help the accountants find the software they needed to update their tracking system.

For another eight months, Brodsky continued to give the firm advice and hammered out the specific terms of a possible deal. Meanwhile, the prospect was also negotiating with its competitor. "In the end, our patience was rewarded," reports Brodsky. "We landed the account."

**85**
**IDEA**

# Tour Turns Visitors into Buyers

**S**med International, a maker of office furniture in Calgary, Alberta, has built sales of US$108 million with no advertising, direct mail, or telemarketing. And compared to its larger rivals, such as Steelcase and Herman Miller, it has no retail presence. So how does Smed do it?

President and CEO Mogens Smed is convinced that an **uncensored demonstration of a product in actual use** can be a company's strongest selling tool. Each month, employees who have worked at Smed for at least two years guide between 15 and 150 visitors through the company's offices, where constantly changing displays of furniture, designed for growing companies, are tagged with vital statistics for quick customer reference. Smed customizes the tour based on what visitors want: Some groups follow the order process through the office, while others get a full factory tour.

A tour of Smed International's bustling plant proves so intoxicating to prospects—who wish their own companies were as energized, profitable, and growing—that few can resist buying the furniture. Mogens Smed claims that 99% of the "tourists" buy from his company.

The tour accomplishes two important goals: It shows off the functionality of Smed furniture better than a static retail window display, and it allows prospects to experience the company's culture. Says one customer, "What they're selling is the Smed way. They're leading the same life as their customers."

**IDEA**

# Use the Pay Phone

**S**weetwater Sound, a seller of audio equipment based in Fort Wayne, Ind., has survived quite well without an 800 number. Although Sweetwater has three retail stores, most of its loyal customers—and there are thousands, including Elton John, Dolly Parton, and Kenny Rogers—buy from the company over the telephone. So why doesn't Sweetwater use the tried-and-true promotional gimmick of a toll-free call?

Chuck Surack, founder of the *Inc.* 500 company that racked up sales of $31 million in 1997, has a few **good reasons for not offering toll-free phone calls**. First, it's a good filter. "If they call on their own nickel, they are pretty darn serious," reasons Surack. Second, an 800 number tends to bring in bargain shoppers who are calling around to find the lowest price on an item and generally aren't interested in building a long-term relationship with the company. Third, the toll charge incurred by the customer is minute compared to the average sale of $1,000 that the company makes over the phone, so an 800 number is really not much of a promotional device. And fourth, it's a sales-control mechanism. "If we had an 800 number, we probably couldn't have kept up with the incoming call volume, so we didn't want to increase it," he explains.

# 87
**IDEA**

# Traffic Jam

**D**ay in and day out, Norman's Optical, in Marblehead, Mass., sells prescription eyeglasses, contact lenses, and sunglasses. But on one July weekend, 250,000 patriotic Americans descended upon the quaint little town to celebrate the USS *Constitution*'s bicentennial sail into its historic harbor. So owner Norman Marquis **took advantage of the extra foot traffic by gearing up for the crowds**.

Marquis turned his subdued optical emporium into sunglasses central for the bright summer weekend. To draw passers-by into the store, sidewalk tables glittered with inexpensive sunglasses, while inside, the top designer brands awaited eager eyes. Marquis ordered early from vendors that sell on consignment, so that he wouldn't be stuck with excess merchandise if his projections were off. In the patriotic spirit, he decorated inside and out with red, white, and blue bunting. "There was definitely a festive feel to the store. Friends and family helped out, and we got catered food to make it fun for the temporary help," says manager Greg Lapham.

Marquis also allowed a few vendors to work the floor and sell samples at discounted prices. "On a good weekend, the company typically sells 8 to 10 pairs of sunglasses," says Lapham. "That day we sold 150. None of the other optical shops in town had thought of this kind of promotion."

**88**
IDEA

# In Search of New Horizons

**A**ccording to Peter Johnstone, former owner of Sunfish/Laser, it's easy to see what markets are growing and vibrant and which ones are in a slump, just by **cruising a variety of trade shows**. The boat show he went to was comparatively depressing, he says. "Boat dealers were more concerned with my new boat's small size than with how it performed. They weren't interested in innovation."

While boat dealers simply plopped their latest model on the floor and stood around waiting for passers-by, the booths at the outdoor-recreation show he attended were much more dramatic, complete with sample white-water runs and ersatz jungles to explore. "It was clear these kayak companies and outdoor-equipment companies had thrived because they weren't sparing any expense on their booths," notes Johnstone. "Crowds gathered around the most experimental water craft."

The trade show helped Johnstone make a major change at his Portsmouth, R.I., company. He unloaded the Sunfish/Laser lines, which were sold through traditional boat distributors, and invested the proceeds in a new company to launch his smaller boat in the dynamic outdoor-recreation market. His choice was a shrewd one. In 1997, Escape Sailboat Co. sold a respectable 1,800 boats and set its sights on 3,400 for 1998.

**IDEA**

# No Drinks on the House

**G**iving a customer free product can do heavy damage to a company's bottom line and doesn't always further a company's growth—especially in two-tier marketing arrangements. Taverns are a perfect example. Many tavern owners routinely squeeze free kegs out of microbreweries anxious to make a sale. Such giveaways have ruined many a microbrew house operating on light profit margins.

Alan Newman, founder and president of the fast-growing Magic Hat Brewery, in Burlington, Vt., borrowed a start-up tactic from the larger, now-established Boston Beer Co. Instead of giving in to demands for free kegs, Magic Hat **offers promotional materials** such as menu tents for tables and coasters that remind customers to order another frosty.

"I am trying to build a customer base, not make a tavern owner richer," says Newman. "To build a customer base, I need to generate more interest in my beer. This is going to help the tavern owner get richer too—just not as fast." Newman has rolled his brand into four states by using dry goods with the Magic Hat logo.

**IDEA**

# Goodwill Garners Repeat Sales

**W**ho says nice guys finish last? Not Iris Harrell of Menlo Park, Calif., who thinks that her thoughtfulness is one reason why repeat customers and referrals amount to 88% of her $3.4-million remodeling company's revenues.

Harrell Remodeling's entire marketing budget is 1% of sales, and she spends 70% of it on **low-cost goodwill efforts that encourage repeat business and generate referrals**. For example, two-thirds of the way into projects involving kitchen remodeling, she sends customers gift certificates for dinner at nearby restaurants, along with a handwritten note apologizing for the inconvenience of having their kitchens ripped apart. She budgets about $3,000 a year for these gifts.

"It's really about creating a positive presence in the community," says Harrell. She also appeals to customers' neighbors by sending "Pardon Our Dust" letters to everyone who lives near a construction site. The letters ask the neighbors to call if there are any noise, trash, or parking problems. Once, three homeowners who lived on the same street did call. Instead of complaining, they asked Harrell to handle their remodeling projects. All three had been referred to her by their neighbors—four past customers of Harrell's.

**91**
**IDEA**

# Start-up Starts with a Contest

**G**athering sales leads is a challenge for a start-up, so it may as well be fun, too. When Deborah Mersino founded Paragon Public Relations, in Evanston, Ill., she sent 120 press releases to business editors nationwide, saying her company wanted to **honor "an unknown entrepreneur" and offer the contest winner a short-term contract**. Entrants had to explain, in five sentences or fewer, why they deserved to be selected. Mersino's campaign caught the attention of three newspapers and a magazine.

As a result, 69 entrepreneurs entered the contest, which cost Paragon only time and postage. One entrant wrote a poem; another composed a song. "I figured that since small-business owners are inherently creative, this campaign would get them to take notice," Mersino says. The winner received a $5,000, six-month contract with Paragon. The runner-up, a Chicago company, got a $1,500 contract. For Paragon, the payoff was lots of press, credibility as a new agency, two clients—and 67 other leads.

# Spiels on Wheels

**M**ost consumer-product manufacturers wouldn't consider trapping prospective customers inside a moving vehicle to deliver a sales pitch, but for three years Boston-based Harpoon Brewery did just that. The microbrewery's van, painted like the company's checkerboard logo, cruised Boston-area streets roughly four out of seven nights a week, carting pedestrians home at no charge. Still, there's no such thing as a completely free ride.

"Once the door closed they were unwitting listeners to the Harpoon propaganda," says company president Rich Doyle. Passengers got information about the $7-million brewery's special events, along with a list of other public-transportation options.

Although the cost of running a moving billboard was not cheap—roughly $4,000 annually, not including the driver's salary and the original cost of the van—the shuttle received positive press that cost a fraction of what a comparable print campaign would cost. **Sponsoring a shuttle service** can create loyal customers and distinguish your company as literally going the extra mile. "It's a public service that reminds people that there are options other than driving home drunk," says Doyle. "It also let people know who we are." Another Boston-area example of motorized promotion: A drugstore chain sends a prominently marked van to cruise highways and help stranded travelers.

# 93
**IDEA**

## Forsaking All Others

**A** sales manager for Leegin Creative Leather Products, based in City of Industry, Calif., once sent a dozen roses to a buyer for a large department-store chain. Courtship? No, more like consolation because he declined the chain's repeated requests for Leegin's handbags.

Leegin Leather has grown since 1980 to more than $100 million a year in revenues by turning down sales from department-store chains. Why? There are two reasons. First, Jerry Kohl, the company's founder and CEO, made a commitment to the specialty stores that originally bet on the company. Second, maintaining healthy cash flow was crucial to his bootstrapping growth strategy, and department stores are known to be late payers. These days, Leegin Leather is large enough to demand better payment terms from department stores, but out of loyalty Kohl **refuses to sell to his core customers' competitors**.

"The loyalty of the specialty shops has made our company profit over the years," explains Kohl, who started out as a boutique owner himself in high school. "There's an old saying: Your company is only as healthy as its customers' business. Well, department stores are notorious for stringing out suppliers, and I knew I couldn't afford that, no matter how large an order they might place with us."

**94
IDEA**

# What Goes Around Comes Around

**P**hyllis Apelbaum, president of $8.1-million Arrow Messenger Service, in Chicago, once said "no, thanks" to a whopping $500,000 sale. "The truth was, we were too small to fulfill the contract," explains Apelbaum. "I knew in good conscience that we couldn't do a good job for these people in the time they needed to have it done."

Apelbaum concedes that when you're first starting out, it's hard to tell anyone, "I'm not going to do your work." But she's a firm believer in manifest destiny: "When you **turn business down for the right reason and in the right way**, very often it will come back to you."

She did, and it did. A few years after the fateful $500,000 decision, Apelbaum got to bid on another large contract: Neiman Marcus was coming to Chicago and needed a courier company. Apelbaum's anecdote about refusing a similar opportunity was a great selling point. She convinced the department store that she understood what it took to service a big account and even offered the other company as a reference.

**IDEA 95**

# Don't Mess with Success

**E**very month, Tom Golisano is faced with a recurring temptation: Should his payroll-processing firm, Paychex, in Rochester, N.Y., jump into the health-insurance business? "We're contacted all the time," he says. Handling the employee deductions would be easy enough. And, he admits, there's a "desire within the company" to add the service.

Still, Golisano resists. "We don't know anything about insurance sales, or we probably know just enough to be dangerous." Health insurance, he notes, is a very volatile product, and the company doesn't have enough expertise to be a competitive force over a long period of time.

Its mission has changed little in 26 years, and for good reason. Because Paychex still owns just a sliver of the market, it makes sense to **keep selling its current line of services rather than take the risk of offering new ones**. With a whopping $500 million in sales but just 5% of the market, there's still plenty of room for the company to grow.

# 96
**IDEA**

# Specialty Shop or Super Mart?

Lynette Hegeman of Danville, Calif., worked for two years to produce a skin cream for pregnant women. She devised the formula with a Stanford dermatologist and consulted with a network of OB-GYN offices. By the time she started to manufacture Belly Butter for stores, her savings were close to being depleted. The business needed a big order right then.

And that's when Hegeman received a visit from a salesman who represented several major retail distributors. He claimed he could take her product across the country in a heartbeat. She knew he had previously been a rep for a major drug company and now made a living discovering new products for mass merchandisers. He'd recently scored with an arthritis cream. The salesman left that day with a jar of Belly Butter, promising to talk to an executive at a large San Francisco distributor that services Wal-Mart and other mass-retail chains.

"He came back to us with a proposal to take our product to mass merchandisers—he could get it into Long's, Wal-Mart, Target, everyplace," and, adds Hegeman, he anticipated a first order of 100,000 units. She was tempted—but she agonized for a month. Pregnant women don't go into Target looking for special skin cream. And, the price would obviously come down. Instead of being upscale, Belly Butter would be just another cream. She also lacked advertising dollars. In the end, Hegeman realized that **appropriate positioning would be more profitable than extensive distribution**: The endorsement of obstetricians and the loyalty of specialty maternity and baby shops were worth more to her future than sitting on the shelf at a discount chain (or worse, the half-off shelf). So she turned down the offer.

# 97
**IDEA**

## Sales: Up for Election

**W**e underestimated the politics behind purchasing decisions in government offices when we started in this business. One of an elected official's primary responsibilities is to stay in office," says a wiser Mike Davis, CEO of The VINE Co., which makes and sells an automated victim-notification service for county and state governments. The Louisville firm discovered that agencies advocating for victims of crime had very little ability to move a sale. As its sales representatives moved up to elected officials like the sheriff or prosecuting attorney, the sale would move forward.

"Doing something for victims is a politically popular agenda item, so our product enjoys bipartisan support," says Davis. Consequently, **sales to government at all levels can be significantly hastened by contacting officials and candidates during election time**. "Then," says Davis, "the official will put more push behind it and speed up the process." For that reason, VINE tracks the political calendar and who is running for office. It focuses its sales and marketing resources accordingly. Result: The company experienced 340% growth in 1997 and is expected to grow 260% in 1998. "When we talk with other companies at trade shows, they say our selling cycle of nine months is very short for the industry. We are constantly working to shorten it," says Davis.

**98**

**IDEA**

# If You've Got It, Flaunt It

Once you commit time and resources to creating a new sales tool, you might as well show it off. That's what MacTemps' Kimberly Kapner did with the CD-ROM she developed to showcase the company's reservoir of graphic design talent. The service company **rolled out its proprietary database at a trade show** the way a product-oriented company would introduce a new model.

Kapner, working out of MacTemps' London office, made a deal with *Creative Technology* (a British industry magazine) to feature the CD-ROM on a cover in the November 1996 issue. The magazine also included a story about the company (which has headquarters in Cambridge, Mass.) and two postcard-insert advertisements that ran over the next few months. Publication coincided with the annual Apple Expo in the United Kingdom, at which both *Creative Technology* and MacTemps had booths. The exposure meant that more of MacTemps' CD-ROMs were given away at the trade show.

"I figured it would be a great way to maximize trade-show coverage," says Kapner, who reports a 30% increase in the number of calls requesting information since the CD-ROM was distributed. Indeed, she adds, "We've had more coverage from this CD-ROM than from anything we've done since we opened the office in London."

**IDEA**

# Take 'Em Out to the Ball Game

Geoff Allen and Jeff Gordon know that filling a room with prospective buyers can be as hard as persuading shortstop Cal Ripken to take a day off. Still, their company, Source Digital Systems—a value-added reseller and integrator of digital video-editing systems headquartered in Vienna, Va.—easily lured 128 fans to their pitch by **inviting hundreds of prospects to one of the season's biggest baseball games**.

The partners rented out an old warehouse next to right field. While the batters warmed up outside, the corporate crowd munched on barbecued chicken inside. Allen and Gordon got the prospects' attention by showing on two large screens how a baseball coach could use the latest video-editing technology for training sessions. The group asked questions and filled out a survey rating the sales presentation and the technology.

Afterward, everyone headed to the stands. The Orioles prevailed—and so did Source Digital. Two months after hosting the $15,000 event (paid for in part by vendor co-op marketing funds), the $12-million company closed six deals worth $420,000. Says Allen, "It was a good day for the clients, for us, and for the Orioles."

**100**
IDEA

# Celebration for Promotion

To lure locals into his restaurants, Jack Baum offers them something hard to resist: a pat on the back. The chairman of Dallas-based Canyon Cafes **sends congratulatory letters and gift certificates to recently promoted area workers**. "Come pop a cork with us," read the personalized greetings, which offer free champagne or wine at any of Baum's 19 restaurants.

The letters bring in lots of new business with little effort or expense. For 45 minutes a day, an administrator combs through local newspapers for promotion announcements, finds employers' addresses, and mails about 30 letters. Baum estimates the program cost $1,625 in 1995 while generating a 29% response rate and $106,177 in revenues. He also figures that each new customer returns three times per year.

By coding the letters he can track the companies whose employees respond most often. The program was so popular with Southwest Airlines employees that Baum called its head office and traded $2,000 worth of dinner passes for $2,000 worth of round-trip tickets to New Orleans and Phoenix. He then held a contest for his employees and customers. Customers, however, were only offered a chance for a trip to Phoenix, where Canyon Cafes has a restaurant. "I wasn't about to send them to a place where we didn't have one," says Baum.

# A Year of Working Successfully

**T**he best promotional pieces are the ones that meet several sales and marketing objectives at once—like Munton's. For more than 40 years, this British producer of malt has spent the lion's share of its marketing budget on a customized desk calendar that goes beyond the predictable scenic photos and company logo. Its leather-bound edition, containing 12 essays written by managers at Munton's, is distributed to key personnel at breweries, distilleries, confectionery companies, and to food giants such as Nestlé. "The quality of the calendar communicates that we are a quality supplier," says Andrew Shelley, group managing director of marketing.

While the essays give customers around the globe a close-up look at what's happening at the company, the writing assignment also gives managers a break from their routines—and motivates them during the year to accomplish something worth reporting in the calendar. One essay, by a food-industry marketing manager, tells about the company's pioneering effort to introduce malt as an ice-cream flavor in South America; another describes the leading-edge agricultural techniques that provide a consistent supply of high-quality product.

Each essay is accompanied by a professional photograph. "This **calendar helps bring the company to life for our customers throughout the year**," says Laurence Moses, senior sales director, who adds that it also distinguishes Munton's as a premium source of malt.

The company prints 1,000 calendars at a cost of $15,000. In addition, as major corporations become increasingly strict about the types of items their buyers can receive during the holiday season, its calendar is a safe gift.

# Free and Easy

To promote your company, you don't have to spend big bucks for small gift items like pens and baseball caps. Sometimes you can **use your existing cache of products and artwork as freebies**.

Linda Reimer, president of Design Basics, a house-plan publisher based in Omaha, discovered two promotional items hiding in her company's inventory. She gives black-and-white illustrations to builders who buy a set of Design Basics plans to use as camera-ready artwork for newspaper advertising. "This makes it easier for builders to pop an ad in local papers to sell our homes. And it helps Design Basics control its image in the marketplace," says Reimer. Duplicating the artwork costs only $5 a shot.

Another inventive promotional item was born at a meeting with key customers: pocket-size blueprints for builders to use as a quick-reference guide when visiting a job site. The $15 expense of shrinking and photocopying key drawings is incidental compared to the convenience it offers builders who aren't personally working on the site. "We are always looking for things we can tack on for free that will make it easier for our brokers to use and sell our product," says Reimer. This is clearly a blueprint for success—sales topped $4 million in 1997.

**103**
IDEA

## Racy Entertainment

**M**ixing business and pleasure isn't necessarily a bad thing. Henry Camferdam Jr., president of Indianapolis-based Support Net, claims that his company's accelerated **growth rate is directly tied to his hobby**.

Camferdam, who is a professional race-car driver, saw potential for building camaraderie between clients and salespeople by sharing his passion for speed. He points out that we all need to blow off steam; we become closer to people with whom we blow off steam, and we become more trusting of them. And how better to blow off steam than to drive really, really fast? So as part of an annual incentive program, the remarketer of IBM computers sends about 20 clients and eight employees to driver-training school. In addition to increasing his company's revenues, Camferdam has gained brand recognition through the race-car program: Resellers who buy from him have no problem distinguishing Support Net from the 15 other IBM distributors with whom it competes.

**104**
**IDEA**

# Money Grows on Shoe Trees

**M**ike Larkin, president of the $20-million Border Cafe restaurants, used to bring two pairs of shoes to the airport when he dropped off or picked somebody up. "It was the only time I could get my shoes shined," he says. His entrepreneur's sixth sense kicked in, and he realized that he was on to something. While scouting El Paso for ideas to bring back to his five-restaurant chain, Larkin came across Kenny Schultz, "the Joe Montana of shoe shines," and hired him as a shoe-shine trainer.

Now, while sipping a margarita and waiting for a table at the Border Cafe, in Saugus, Mass., **customers get extra service**—a free professional shoe shine. "One customer, who owned 102 pairs of shoes, hired one of our shoe-shine people on an independent basis," says Larkin. Is the expense of employing someone just to shine customers' shoes worth it? The results speak for themselves: In an area that has seen the turnover of more than 1,500 restaurants, the Border Cafe in Saugus has been thriving since 1989. Oh, and by the way, while you're savoring a chicken fajita and wiggling your toes inside shiny black boots, it's just possible that one of the valet parkers will be vacuuming your car for free.

**IDEA 105**

# For a Limited Time Only

If your company is struggling with the pendulum swings of the seasons, you may want to rethink your strategy altogether. Calendar Club, in Austin, Tex., opens its doors just three months of the year during the Christmas season. "Many retailers struggle to break even or lose money during the rest of the year," observes president Marc Winkelman, who has grown the chain of gift stores to a hefty $65 million since 1992 by **shortening the selling season** to maximize return on investment.

The Calendar Club capitalizes on vacant store space and rented kiosks in malls. While this real estate can cost as much as $200 per square foot for three months during the holidays—$30,000 to $40,000 for a premium mall space—that's still less expensive than renting the space and keeping it open the other nine months of the year. Another key to making the strategy work is a big investment in a point-of-purchase information system that can maintain order during the crush at the cash register during a chaotic selling season. Calendar Club maintains a staff of regional managers to recruit and staff the stores with battle-tested retail clerks who are capable of handling the preholiday intensity.

The company's counterintuitive strategy has been so successful that in 1995 a major bookstore chain went into competition against Calendar Club, snagging prime store space because the bookstore already maintained a permanent presence in malls. To stay on equal footing, Calendar Club sold stock to another bookstore chain that also rents space in malls year-round.

# 106
**IDEA**

## In the Flesh

For years we were coming in second all the time when competing against the heavyweights," laments Lee Kirkwood, CEO of United Mail, a Louisville company that provides mailroom-management services. Kirkwood investigated and discovered that competing proposals closely resembled his own. The résumés of mailroom managers assigned to work at a customer's site were also competitive.

So Kirkwood decided to **differentiate his company by bringing along the individual who would be working on-site for the client**, rather than just the person's résumé. The tactic told prospects that United Mail was really serious about getting their business. Plus, prospects could meet the person who would be working there and for whom they would be paying. Introducing the proposed on-site manager is now the company's standard operating procedure when calling on customers from Pittsburgh to New Orleans. While Kirkwood hasn't kept track of how many sales have closed as a result, the company's volume grew to $25 million in 1997.

# 107
**IDEA**

## Bring Out the Big Guns

IBM became legendary for impressing large corporate clients by calling on them with a team of salespeople, each member an expert in one of the customer's particular computing needs. Small companies without an enormous sales force can **look bigger and more experienced by hiring a consultant part-time to go along on sales calls**.

Beth Armknecht, owner of MA&A Group, a $4-million information-systems consulting firm in Atlanta, went one step further and hired someone full-time from a prominent consulting company to add depth to her sales team. "There are a lot of people who are sick of traveling and are willing to take a reduction in pay to avoid the travel," she observes.

Other small companies bring along salespeople from big-name suppliers who will be involved in filling the order. Bill Theriault, vice-president of Precision Components, in Peterborough, N.H., observes, "as much as a big-name client likes you and your company, chances are they like doing business with another big brand name more."

**IDEA**

# Riskless Business

**W**hen you own a small, growing company, the secret to overcoming sales resistance—or, better yet, making sure potential objections never come up—is to address them subtly in your company's marketing materials. For example, MTS-Group, a recruiting business in Waltham, Mass., **offers more than the classic money-back guarantee**. The company tells potential customers that if they're not completely satisfied with its résumé-database service in 60 days, they'll get six months of free job-posting advertising on the Internet, in addition to their money back. Of course, the company takes precautions to make sure customers won't need to use the guarantee, according to president Dan Miller. To assure satisfaction with the database, MTS asks some new customers to take a brief training program so that they know how to use it effectively.

# Shifting Terrain

**W**hen Polaris Industries, a snowmobile manufacturer in Minneapolis, rolled out its first all-terrain vehicle (ATV), it was entering a market already dominated by Honda, the giant with an 80% share. Suzuki, Yamaha, and Kawasaki shared the rest of the market. These companies all targeted thrill-seeking teenagers.

To open up the market, Polaris **reassessed potential uses for the product and pitched it to a new set of buyers**: people looking for a good way to haul firewood and do other outdoor chores too big for a wheelbarrow but not big enough for a full-blown tractor. Ads for the "utility vehicle" were placed in hunting and fishing magazines, publications aimed at motor sports enthusiasts, and in periodicals for farmers. The strategy worked: ATV sales now account for 45% of Polaris's revenues, and the company now claims the second largest market share, just behind Honda.

**110**

IDEA

# Way Kewl Tactic, Dude

**T**raditional software markets wouldn't be able to reach the target customers for "Let's Talk about ME!"—the first CD-ROM from Girl Games, in Austin, Tex., geared specifically to teenage and preteen girls. President and CEO Laura Groppe had done enough intensive research and focus groups—nail painting at slumber parties, shopping, and wrapping houses in toilet paper—to know that girls 8 to 16 years old weren't hanging out in computer stores.

So the company aggressively **sought alternative merchandisers**—the ones that didn't traditionally sell computer games but would expose "Let's Talk" to the girls for whom the product was intended. Groppe turned to retailers such as Contempo Casuals and the clothing store Wet Seal—stores that interested her focus groups when she took them shopping at the mall.

"Girls that age are a lot more independent," says Jann Baskett, vice-president of marketing at Girl Games. "Single-parent and dual-income households have created a young consumer who is making more and more decisions for the household—and now is making more money herself, through baby-sitting or whatever." And she's not spending that money, nearly 100% of which is disposable income, in computer stores. Contempo Casuals and Wet Seal reportedly sell 80% of the "Let's Talk" CD-ROMs they receive, which confirms the effectiveness of Groppe's distribution strategy.

# Scientific Evidence Sells

**Y**our product is technologically advanced but difficult to explain. How do you sell it? Optiva, maker of an electronic toothbrush that uses sound waves traveling through fluid to clean teeth, **includes a tome of scientific research in its sales proposal**. That's because the proposal goes to dentists, who are accustomed to reading scientific research digests.

Optiva, based in Bellevue, Wash., pours 5% of its revenues back into research and development, not only for setting up its own labs but also for funding dental research on the Sonicare toothbrush at Harvard, Northwestern, and Tufts universities, among others. Some 47 papers on the Sonicare's effectiveness were published in dental journals, which, bundled together, make a satisfying *whump* when dropped by a salesperson onto a dentist's desk.

"Our goal was always to get the dentists to try the Sonicare," says cofounder David Giuliani. "If we got that, we'd win their recommendation." It's working: Optiva holds 40% of the market for electric toothbrushes sold directly from dental practices.

**IDEA**

# Tuned to Their Needs

**F**letcher Music Centers, in Clearwater, Fla., used to sell keyboard instruments and nothing else. Today it does all it can to meet the musical, physical, and social needs of its primary customers, retirees. Since 1986, president John Riley has reworked every aspect of customer service—from designing a home organ with oversize print and controls to making free group lessons a social event.

To succeed at value-added selling, Riley **organized his entire company around serving customers**. His first goal was to get regional managers to buy in and spread the word to retail stores. At the same time, he was mobilizing employees through focus groups and monthly open sales meetings.

Riley would select two Employees of the Month for customer service—one from sales and one from customer support (including administration, service, and delivery). Winners got $250 and their names on a company plaque. Recognizing all levels of customer-service achievement helped foster goodwill between sales and support. It also rewarded salespeople "in front of their peers for something other than selling" and made providing exemplary customer service an integral part of the company's culture. Best of all, it boosted sales: In recent years, Fletcher's sales have almost quadrupled, to $40 million, despite a long decline in the organ market.

**113**

**IDEA**

# Cast into the Past

**T**hese days, Orvis Co., the upscale outfitter founded in 1856 and based in Manchester, Vt., sells more clothing and gifts than its original stock-in-trade—fishing and hunting gear. But "without our fly-fishing heritage," says catalog manager Tom Rosenbauer, "we'd be just another rag vendor."

To reel in new generations of loyal customers, the company **markets its long history by offering classes** in fly-fishing. These classes run for two to three days, cost $350 to $400, and are held in beautiful, trout-stocked waters. Instructors teach enthusiasts a variety of casting styles, how to assemble a reel, and basic fish behavior, without boring them with long-winded sales pitches. Not every student buys a rod and reel, which can cost upward of $500, but some might spring for a shirt as they fondly remember their days of fishing. The strategy works: Orvis sells more than $350 million a year, and its customers know they are buying from "the best in the business."

**IDEA**

# Fly-in Tours

**R**ite-Hite, a Milwaukee manufacturer of loading-dock equipment, **uses a fly-in program to educate users and customers' quality and safety teams**. When guests tour the factory, they kick the tires of some 100 pieces of equipment, including about 40 models from Rite-Hite's competitors.

The tour helps visitors identify their needs and explore possible solutions. More than 90% of fly-in prospects eventually buy from Rite-Hite, says Robert Staehler, the program's director. He says that representatives of more than 200 companies participate in Rite-Hite's fly-in tours annually. In 1991, a banner year, 353 companies visited, and within 12 months they had purchased $12 million worth of equipment. Costs, including follow-up after that year's tours, totaled $250,000. The big payoff: Rite-Hite's sales soared from about $40 million in 1988 (the year the tours started) to about $250 million in 1997. Staehler says a sizable portion of the growth is a result of the fly-in program. His advice:

  *Start small.* Invite only those who will influence the buying decision. Stock a few key competitors' products, and expand as you grow.

  *Share the cost.* In 1988, Rite-Hite invited just 37 companies and paid the entire travel bill; now it pays half, and the sales reps pick up the other half for their customers.

  *Set benchmarks.* "A minimum 50% closing ratio is good if you keep costs in line," says Staehler. "If you can't meet that, stay with more traditional marketing."

  *Skip the frills.* "This doesn't have to be lavish," he says. "They come because they're scared of making the wrong decision."

# Call on an Impulse

It wasn't until Nick Molina got desperate that he found out he was selling his product in the wrong places.

Molina, cofounder and CEO of Let's Talk Cellular and Wireless, a Miami-based retailer of phones and pagers, started out by hawking his products from a customized van. The concept of a store with four on the floor showed steady promise until one of Molina's big customers, which was some $200,000 in arrears, went under.

In a last-ditch effort to save his company, Molina set up a **sales booth in the midst of heavy traffic—foot traffic**—under a tent at an outdoor auto race. The impulse to sell there proved right. Customer response was overwhelming. He and his partners concluded that cellular phones might actually be an impulse purchase. They also realized that there are ready-made meccas for impulse buyers: shopping malls.

Armed with the discovery that Let's Talk Cellular had been missing out on the best market for its product, the company negotiated kiosk space in a Miami mall and rang up record sales there. The company now operates in 89 malls in 13 states and Puerto Rico.

**116**
**IDEA**

# Trading on Your Size

**D**espite a start-up's drive to grow, being small is not always a liability from the customer's perspective. In 1994, Thompson Doyle & Co. was a four-year-old, $1-million real-estate brokerage in Boston, competing for a long-term contract against rivals 25 times its size. "We were up against every other brokerage in the city," recalls cofounder Catherine Thompson. She and her partner **turned smallness into an asset with the message, "You'll be a big fish in a small pond."** Thompson says they used all the traditional sales tactics, but they ultimately won the contract by proving they had the most to gain—therefore, they would make the customer's project a top priority. One year later, Thompson Doyle's sales had more than doubled.

# 117
**IDEA**

# The High Price of Free Stuff

**N**ew entrepreneurs are often warned against giving away product to get a business off the ground. But some of the most successful companies have gotten rich giving away their products. **So, if you're rethinking the giveaway, here are some questions to ask yourself.**

*Are you likely to work with this customer again?* The Rosen Group, in Baltimore, earns $4 million annually providing an array of services for craftspeople. It provides free, basic business advice to artists via an 800 number to expose prospects to its wide variety of services.

*Are your costs for each additional unit low?* For example, in the software industry duplicating a program costs very little. Therefore, many companies can afford to give their core product away as shareware. Users only pay if they like the product and want additional services, like technical support and documentation.

*Are customers balking at trying your unusual, unknown, or complex product?* Not long ago, Maurice Lepenven, Northeast regional sales manager of Quantum Electronics, in Warwick, R.I., was having trouble selling his air-purification systems due to their $700 to $900 price tags. Free trial offers proved just the ticket to educating prospects about the mysterious units, driving 1997 sales to $1.35 million.

*Can you trade a freebie for something you want more?* Since 1996, SBT Accounting Systems, in San Rafael, Calif., has been selling software that enables electronic commerce on Web sites. Its most powerful marketing strategy was an offer to set up a Web page free for any chamber of commerce in the country, in exchange for access to its members.

**IDEA**

# Selling by Design

**S**teve Ettridge, founder and CEO of Temps & Co., a temporary- and permanent-placement company in Washington, D.C., sells at "both ends" of his business. He sells to businesses who need employees, and he sells his company to the employees he places. By the mid-1990s, Ettridge realized that the biggest obstacle to growth was a shortage of temps, not clients.

"The minute you conceive of the temp as your real customer," says Ettridge, "everything changes—right down to the space in which you do business." So the company started asking prospective temps about the places they hang out. "It turns out," he says, "they shop, they go to the movies, and they go to Starbucks."

Based on this feedback, Ettridge decided to **redesign his offices to "make applying for a job as simple and inviting as ordering a cup of coffee."** The solution was the Job Store, a walk-in retail location where the trendy decor—round tables, counters, stools, mirrors, and designer lighting—mimics a bistro or perhaps the cosmetics section of a department store. By the second half of 1998, Ettridge expected to have three Job Stores operating in the D.C. area, and the impact of the redesign has been substantial. After Temps & Co. redesigned its first location, recruitment at that site increased 25%.

**119**

**IDEA**

# The Taste of Success

**G**etting prospective consumers to try a new product is 99% of the challenge for sales. CEO Bob Stiller of Green Mountain Coffee, in Waterbury, Vt., puts it this way: "We'll never be able to compete with Maxwell House's advertising budget, but if we can get someone to taste our coffee, then we'll probably gain a loyal customer." So Green Mountain negotiated the right to sell coffee by the cup in the bakery area of a major chain's supermarkets. Once customers sampled the product and the company demonstrated that it could build a customer base, it was easier to get on the shelves.

**Sampling in retail outlets** became a key part of the premium roaster and distributor's growth strategy in 1993, when it had $10 million in sales. Casting about for ways to grow, Stiller struck up a relationship with a local gas station/convenience store to sell coffee by the cup. The owner didn't really believe Green Mountain could make it, since Dunkin' Donuts had an outlet across the street. To make sure his coffee would survive this worst-case scenario, Stiller assigned an employee to train the convenience-store staff to brew fresh pots regularly and make sure the bagged coffee was being displayed properly—detail-merchandising techniques considered indispensable even today.

To the convenience-store owner's surprise and Stiller's delight, the coffee not only sold briskly, it also increased traffic to the gas station. Armed with this initial success, Stiller struck deals to sell his coffee at 1,000 Mobil stations around the country.

**120**

**IDEA**

# If It Hollers, Let It Go

**W**hen you sell more to existing customers, be sure the additional sales are profitable. If not, you may have to **turn down sales that don't leverage your company's core skills and assets**. Look at what happened to Taylor Management Systems, a $13-million company in Des Plaines, Ill., that contracts out software developers and technicians to large corporations. Motorola Cellular was its profitable and steady customer. "We support Motorola Cellular's entire help desk," says president Janet Taylor. When Motorola Cellular wanted to outsource its telephone operation—a bank of live operators—Taylor Management agreed to take it on.

"It turned out to be a total nightmare," says Taylor. "What did we really know about telephone operators who make $7 an hour, versus $40,000-a-year professional technicians? The turnover was just tremendous." Every time one of the phone operators quit, Taylor had to find a replacement that day, forcing her to hire temps for only a dollar less per hour than she was billing Motorola. As a result, with costs soaring, Taylor's profit on the account took a beating.

A year later, when the phone contract was up for renewal, Motorola offered to expand it. Taylor passed, and instead she found a good replacement temp agency to smooth the transition. She retained the part of the Motorola business that had been profitable to her.

# It's Who You Know

**D**avid Sluter, CEO of $6-million New England Construction, in Rumford, R.I., recently carried out a preconstruction service agreement for a family-owned business whose patriarch he respected. But, during the course of the work, the patriarch's son took on an increasing managerial role. "Junior," as Sluter took to referring to him, was being groomed to take over. However, his inexperience working with suppliers became painfully obvious. New England Construction got paid, but not without a dispute over the deal.

Finally, "Junior" canceled his plans for a new building and decided to renovate instead. Sluter was asked to bid, but he'd had enough, and he is wary of future dealings with his old customer. "I don't want to commit a project manager to something that might become a heartache. It's a risky business as it is," he says. The lesson he learned: Make sure that you **know who you'll be working with and maintain a healthy working relationship with that person**, so that you can reduce your risk as much as possible. If that doesn't happen, says Sluter, "Get out."

# "You Oughta Be in Pictures"

**U**rban Juice & Soda, in Vancouver, B.C., has learned that **enchanted customers are its greatest salespeople**. The company uses photos sent in by customers on the labels of its Jones Soda. And company founder Peter van Stolk is betting that those customers will tell their friends.

Having a picture of your customer's Doberman in roller skates on the Venice Beach boardwalk generates a buzz around the product and encourages all of the pup's friends to buy the soda; it also saves money on label art. The product gets a truly original, customer-centered package, and since the pictures change frequently, soda drinkers can look forward to a surprise before gulping on a hot summer's day. "I can't tell you Jones is cool," says van Stolk. "You have to hear it from someone you think is cool."

# IV

"The more the customer needs your knowledge, the more value you bring to the relationship. The price you command is a function of the value you deliver."

**KEVIN DAVIS**
sales consultant,
Danville, Calif.

# Flexible Fees

**P**atty DeDominic, CEO of $19-million PDQ Personnel Services, in Los Angeles, knows how tough it can be to run a profitable business. PDQ's original pricing model was simple: Charge a recruitment fee for permanent employees, and charge by the hour for temporary placements. When the job market shrank a few years ago, however, PDQ **negotiated each contract individually**. Its clients were hiring less frequently and were more likely to use contingency workers for projects, whether they lasted a few weeks or several years. Here's DeDominic's advice about pricing for that market.

&. *Set parameters*. DeDominic provides guidelines, not inflexible rules. The 13 employees who price contracts know that costs are about 30% above direct labor, and so they add a markup of 30% (for breakeven) to 80%—depending on length of assignment, risk factors, and client.

&. *Get a second opinion*. When she hired an accounting firm to do a top-down review of PDQ's strategy, DeDominic found that too often her company was pricing long-term projects at the same level as short-term. Now PDQ discounts the rate on its longer-term, more lucrative services and increases their value to customers.

## Serious Buyers Only

**S**ometimes the customers you can make the most profit margin from are the most risky," says Charlie Broadway, a lumber broker in Greensboro, N.C. "Either they can't buy from someone else because other suppliers have perceived the risk too, or their credit's been cut off." He should know—he learned the hard way. His company, Spartan Forest Products, has been the victim of nonpaying customers so often that he takes out indemnity insurance.

Broadway is talking about prospects without a referral from anyone in his network of contacts—such as a speculator who is trying to put a deal together for a client but doesn't have a firm order yet. He **quotes high prices to people who call out of the blue**. If the prospects want to buy anyway, that's a red flag that says they probably don't have any money. That kind of calculation and precaution has helped grow Spartan: In its first five years, sales sprouted from $723,000 to $12.6 million.

# More Nights at the Opera

**A**fter a rough season, the Washington Opera Co., in Washington, D.C., thought about raising ticket prices again. However, after carefully reviewing ticket-sales history, manager Jimmy Legarreta realized that the box office routinely turned people away on Friday and Saturday nights, while tickets for midweek performances went unsold. Apparently, all theater seats are not equal.

Legarreta had stumbled onto a system practiced religiously by airlines, called "yield management": maximizing revenue by **pricing tickets according to the demand for each seat at each show time**.

To put his theory into effect, Legarreta and his staff sat in every one of the opera house's 2,200 seats and gave each a value based on the view and the acoustics. With his revenue goal in mind, he played with ticket prices until he arrived at nine different levels, up from five. In the end, the Washington Opera raised prices for its most coveted seats by as much as 50%, but it also dropped the prices of some 600 less desirable tickets. The end result was affordable opera for more people, as well as a 9% revenue increase during the following season.

**126**
**IDEA**

# Holding Back on Price Hikes

In today's tough business environment, imposing an outright price increase can put an account in jeopardy. However, there are other ways to adjust your cost-price ratio when profit margins shrink. **Ask customers to absorb charges for ancillary services** associated with your company's product or service. Jim Roberts, owner of $6.7-million American Express Regency Travel and Cruise, in Ontario, Calif., got good results when he tried it. He asked his 50 core corporate customers to pick up the tab for overnight mail and other deliveries. It was either that, he explained, or charge delivery fees for each transaction. Surprisingly, only two clients refused to help out. Many even offered their own overnight-delivery account numbers. The result: Roberts's delivery costs dropped from more than $300 a month to $50.

# Breaking through the Size Barrier

**Y**ou're small. You're unknown. Why should we take a chance on you?" That's the sales resistance entrepreneurs love to hate—and you may have heard it a thousand times. When a potential customer questions your company's stability and capability, no pat answer will do. In fact, the way you respond to doubts can determine your future with some buyers.

Eric Schechter, founder of Great American Events, a $2.2-million event-marketing company in Scottsdale, Ariz., wasted no time before making his early customers the springboard of his first marketing campaign: He granted his first big-name accounts **certain price concessions in exchange for endorsements**. "I asked if we could use their photos in our print ads, video, and direct-mail pieces," he says. In return for better terms, the customers agreed to be photographed and filmed and to take dozens of calls from prospects who saw their faces plastered on brochures. "The testimonials made us seem bigger than we were right away," Schechter says. "They broke that barrier of newness."

**128**

**IDEA**

# A Grand by Any Other Name

**C**ash up front" is a great term to include in a sales contract, but how do you convince a customer to go for it? Yehoram Uziel, founder of Soligen, in Northridge, Calif., tapped three potential customers he calls "alpha partners" for **"membership fees to share in our technology."**

Uziel's $5.5-million company builds machines that can quickly turn computer designs into ceramic molds for metal casting. The three "alpha partners" get basic versions of Soligen's machine and technical support on an exclusive basis for 6 to 12 months. In exchange, they supply up-front cash (at least $200,000 each) and regular input into the commercial product's design specifications.

When the commercial product is ready to sell, the original partners have no ongoing rights to the technology, says Uziel, but they can buy it exclusively, cutting out their competitors' access to it. "And spiritually, we remember them as the people who took a risk when nobody else would."

**129 IDEA**

# Slow Boat to Payment

**M**ost companies assume that a slow payer or a bad credit risk is not worth selling products or services to, but that's not necessarily true," notes Les Kirschbaum, president/CEO of Mid-Continent Agencies, an accounts-receivable management firm based in Rolling Meadows, Ill. "If you can **negotiate the right credit terms and interest charges up front**, you can make a sale to a slow payer pay off." His suggestions:

🕿 *Develop a payment profile of customers before any sale,* using your accounts-receivable records. If you can predict, based on past performance, that a company won't pay you before 90 days elapse, price the transaction at a high enough level to cover that payment delay.

🕿 *Require slow payers to agree to added interest charges.* Just tacking a surcharge onto each month's bill won't help if your customers ignore it. But requiring them to sign a contractual agreement early on will improve your chances of collecting the full bill eventually, especially if a lawsuit proves necessary.

🕿 *Track slow-paying customers closely.* Make certain your receivables records can tell you when to expect your payment. Then, urges Kirschbaum, if your records tell you 60 days and it's Day 61, your collection staffers need to get on the phone and start soliciting the payment. Remember, some slow payers eventually default on their debts and go out of business.

# Check, Mate

**W**hile many salespeople ask prospects for cash up front, they often cave in to a customer's demands for better payment terms. Not so at Smed International, an office-interiors manufacturer in Calgary, Alberta. CEO Mogens Smed wins the dickering match by pulling out **photocopies of big deposit checks from other customers**. By now he has a thick stack from well-known companies. Smed's little trick helped his 15-year-old company rack up sales of US$108 million in 1997.

# Value vs. Vision

If you're in the consulting business, you're all too familiar with this question: "What do you charge; what's your day rate?" How you answer often determines whether you make the sale, and it affects your overall success. The price you set is not just a financial issue. It's a marketing issue that determines how you position yourself and how the market perceives you.

**Name a price at the outset and "you're dead,"** says Tom McNeil, president of Executive Career Resource Group, a Wellesley, Mass., firm that advises executives and consultants. "You'll only get talked down and never talk yourself up." Here's what else can happen:

1. Your price is too high, and you knock yourself out of the game.
2. Your price is much less than the client was prepared to pay, and you lose money.
3. Your price is much less than that of your competitors, and you are perceived as offering less value.
4. The client accepts your price but then decides that your services aren't worth it, because you haven't convinced him or her of your value.

Many consultants determine their fees by deciding how much money they want to make on an annual basis, then work backwards by figuring the number of billable days in a year to determine an hourly or day rate. But this is "amateurish and self-limiting," argues Alan Weiss, author of *Million Dollar Consulting* (McGraw-Hill, 1997, $29.95), considered by many to be the "bible" of consulting. Instead, says Weiss, the way to become wealthy is to base fees on the client's perceived value of your assistance. Make the conceptual sale first, then attach a value to it—and ask for it.

# Terms of Endearment

One of the toughest subjects a salesperson must discuss with a prospect is payment terms. It's so tough, in fact, that many salespeople just skip it altogether, hoping they won't lose their commission if the customer turns out to be a deadbeat. To make sure your reps aren't disappointed, **don't sign on new customers until they've agreed to your payment terms**.

Patty DeDominic, CEO and president of PDQ Personnel Services, a $19-million placement firm in Los Angeles, credits that policy with saving her from having to call in a collection agency. "We spell out our terms and ask new customers in advance whether those terms fit their internal policies. When there's a conflict, we try to work out an acceptable compromise. Then we follow up with a written document reiterating our terms."

**IDEA**

# Two-Wheeler Dealer

**W**hen Chris Zane learned at a trade show that some bicycle shops were offering five-year warranties on new bikes, he one-upped the competition by **offering a lifetime service guarantee**. "I figured that for most people, five years is the life of the bike," says the president of $1.7-million Zane's Cycles, in Branford, Conn. "If they've had it for longer, they're probably not riding it that much." Zane draws comfort from numbers. He says that everyone uses the free service the first year they have the bike, but only 20% to 30% come back the second year. At that rate, his liability for lifetime free service would be minuscule. "We wanted to make our existing customers apostles," says Zane, who also makes it a practice not to charge customers for parts costing less than a dollar. And when it's time for a new bike, Zane expects to get first shot at the sale.

# Promises, Promises?

**H**ere's an all-too-common business scenario: A salesperson snags a contract for a long-term project at a profitable price, but the delivery date is totally unrealistic. Havoc ensues, and work falls behind schedule, frustrating the customer and ruining any chances for repeat business.

Bay Cast, a steel foundry in Bay City, Mich., makes it its mission to **honor every delivery date it promises customers**. "In our industry, you become a hero because no one does it," says CEO Scott L. Holman, whose company has maintained a 99% on-time delivery rate since he bought this casualty of the Rust Belt in 1989. "I know, because I'm on the board of the Steel Founders Society of America, and we run some surveys on what customers complain about. Those of us who succeed make sure we meet our deadlines."

To keep his company's promise, Holman borrowed a scheduling technique used by NASA. No sales proposal goes out until the production manager assesses resources and builds the proposed project into the foundry's production schedule, committing to a set of internal deadlines. Contingency time is also built into the delivery dates.

Bay Cast's in-depth approach may result in schedules that aren't always what the customer wants to hear. "Sometimes we lose sales because a competitor promises a delivery date we know is unrealistic," notes Holman. "We'll mark a date on our calendar to call the lost prospect back and ask how an order has turned out. Inevitably, it hasn't received its shipment, and we'll convert the prospect into our customer." And this company has certainly succeeded. Sales have grown to $15 million since Holman embarked on the turnaround.

**135**

**IDEA**

# Cast in Concrete

**B**etsy Wiersma's clients ranged from large corporations to the mayor of Indianapolis. Her company, $1.5-million Wiersma Event Marketing, once put on a city festival for 30,000 people. She draws the line, however, with would-be customers who can't (or won't) define their business goals.

A large corporation all but begged Wiersma to take on its trade-show booth. It was a major show, and the budget was considerable. However, the corporation didn't want to talk details: It wouldn't define what it wanted the show to accomplish or how much traffic it expected the booth to generate. Its attitude was "read my mind," recalls Wiersma. When a customer dictates "Just do it!" it's a sure sign that time-consuming and expensive changes will be necessary after the planning stage is over.

Another company might have jumped at the challenge—and the money. Regardless of how forthcoming a customer is with fees, Wiersma **refuses to sign on until concrete goals and timelines are hammered out in writing**. She must have done something right; in January 1998, Wiersma sold her company to St. Louis-based Creative Producers Group.

# 136
**IDEA**

## Fleeter Meter

**V**incent Yost, founder of Intelligent Devices, in Harleysville, Pa., was having a tough time trying to get city officials to buy the expensive, high-tech parking meters his company sells. To let them experience the earning power of his new machines, Yost arranged to give a few towns free trials. But because the towns were allowed to keep the additional revenue that the trial meters were generating, they had zero incentive to speed up the bid process and actually buy the meters.

To keep potential buyers motivated, an industry colleague urged Yost to **contractually claim the revenues generated by the free trial meters**, so that cities would move more quickly toward a purchase. The jury is still out on Yost's experience, but the advice is shrewd: Make sure a free trial offer is just that—and not a free ride for a customer.

# The Shipping News

**B**efore slapping a price tag on your company's best-selling product for a foreign market, it pays to scrutinize the transportation costs associated with delivering goods overseas. After such costs are layered onto the price of your product, it may no longer be competitive in the marketplace. Transportation rates vary widely, depending on such factors as routes, space availability, the type of freight being transported, its volume, the regularity of shipments, and insurance costs. That's why it's best to **quote prices "delivery ex-works" (delivery excluded)**.

"When it comes to delivery, ask customers what kind of shipment they prefer. If delivery charges price your product out of the market, take a stab at trying to find a more competitive rate for the customer," says Spencer Smith, general partner of Business Books Network, an international rep and distribution firm in Dover, N.H. If your company is new to the international market but your customer regularly imports from other companies around the world, it may make sense to piggyback on a transportation network already in place, Smith adds.

**IDEA 138**

## Sold on Delivery

**W**hen selling overseas, your sales reps may find that foreign customers balk at your long delivery times. To prove that it's just as easy and speedy to buy from your company as it is to buy from a local supplier, **give foreign customers the same delivery guarantees** that you give your American customers. That's what the former vice-president of sales and marketing for ELF Machinery discovered when he first called on prospects in the United Kingdom.

"We kept our 10-day delivery promise by shipping by air rather than ocean," says Jeff Ake. "It was really expensive, but it was worth it because it impressed customers and showed them we were serious about selling in their country." After a year, the $25-million company, a manufacturer of bottling equipment in LaPorte, Ind., had built up enough business to justify investing in an overseas warehouse. With warehoused inventory ready to go, ELF saves money by shipping by sea and still keeps its delivery promises.

# Around the World in 30 Days

**C**ongratulations! Your company's plan for global diversification is a wild success, with orders rolling in from around the world. Now you've got to figure out how to get paid without losing sales. Here are some **tips for keeping foreign sales profitable**.

  *Take a conservative stance.* Walk away from any sale that would scare you off at home. Before signing on the bottom line, learn as much as you can about the country's creditor protection laws (if any) and your customer's credit history, as well as payment norms. "Take a country like Malaysia," says Stephen Chipman, director of international services for accounting firm Grant Thornton's southwestern U.S. division, based in Dallas. "If you say COD, Malaysian companies interpret that as meaning payment is due in 30 days. Then you're lucky if they get around to paying you within 90 days." To quantify the risks, check with your regional branch of the Export-Import Bank, as well as the U.S. Chamber of Commerce.

  *Insist on payment in U.S. dollars* to protect against currency risks as well as credit risks—even when customers are in countries that seem safe. If your potential customer won't agree, either take out a letter of credit or move on to the next prospect. Don't delude yourself into thinking you're at risk only in a volatile Eastern European or third-world country.

  *Insure your foreign receivables* if you want to offer flexible terms to avoid losing business, but feel the deal is risky. The Export-Import Bank (202-565-3900) offers a variety of insurance packages, including some aimed at small businesses and short-term buyers of single policies.

**140**

**IDEA**

# Volunteer for the Draft

**C**ompany owners, grateful that a customer has agreed to pay by letter of credit, often think of that document as a bank check, not a statement of the final terms of sale. But how the customer fills in the blanks determines how promptly a supplier gets paid—if at all. "Tell customers that you want to **participate in drafting the letter of credit**," urges Richard Koehler, president of IKR, a $1-million export company based in Houston.

If you tell a customer to "take care of the details," you are effectively surrendering control of the sale. The customer can then tweak the terms in ways the seller never imagined. For instance, a customer may stipulate that payment will be made when goods arrive safely at its foreign warehouse, rather than when the ship leaves port. But a shipwreck could sink the cargo, or the goods might not pass an inspection, and the supplier would have to pay to ship them back to the United States.

One novice, Koehler recalls, typed into the letter of credit the exact weight of the cheese being transported. When the shipment arrived a couple of pounds short because moisture had evaporated, the letter of credit was invalidated. Issuing an amendment cost $300 in bank fees, wiping out the cheese seller's profit. "There's no incentive for the bank issuing the letter of credit to advise its customer, either," says Koehler. "Banks earn fees every time an amendment must be made to the letter of credit." Koehler learned all that the hard way, but now he gladly shares his experience: He teaches classes on how to negotiate international business agreements.

# Letter Perfect Credit

**D**oing business overseas can be riskier than selling domestically, unless you have a shrewd sales representative who can **negotiate an international letter of credit on terms favorable to you**. Sandy Kurz of Compass Forwarding, an international transportation-logistics company based in Jamaica, N.Y., recommends pushing for the following terms when negotiating international letters of credit.

    *Partial shipments.* These are especially useful when a customer is purchasing a large quantity. By asking for the right to send partial shipments, a manufacturer can obtain payment for smaller batches ahead of the final due date to speed up cash flow. "Then you can fill the rest of the order on the customer's nickel," observes Kurz.

    *At-sight clause.* Getting paid "at sight" is about as close to cash as you can get. This means that when all the documents called for by the letter of credit are presented to the bank in charge of releasing payment on behalf of the customer, it will take about five days for the issuing bank to pay it out. Some banks in remote parts of the world may take weeks just to assemble the paperwork before being able to release funds "at sight," so make sure your sales rep qualifies not only the customer but also the customer's bank for the letter of credit.

**142**

**IDEA**

# Worldwide Number-Crunchers

**A**s chief executive of L&R Manufacturing, a Kearney, N.J., company that sells its ultrasonic cleaning machinery and other products overseas, Jim Lazarus used to rely on the advice of a Big Six accounting firm to hammer out sales contracts and payment terms for customers in 52 countries. The accounting firm was great at negotiating the intricacies of each country's unique tariffs, duty rates, and import quotas, but it was too costly and too bureaucratic. Lazarus solved the problem by **switching to a regional accounting firm that was part of an international network**—a good compromise between the sophistication of a Big Six outfit and the hand-holding that comes naturally to partners at smaller ones.

L&R hired one of 140 accounting firms located in 82 countries that make up the Moores Rowland International network. "If we've got a problem or questions about anything to do with an overseas sale, we call our managing partner there. Then, if it's necessary, he'll contact someone at one of the overseas affiliates to handle it," says Lazarus. Clients get charged by both firms at their hourly rates, which are usually cheaper than those of a Big Six firm.

To locate an accounting firm near you that is part of an international accounting network, call the Affiliated Conference of Practicing Accountants International (978-689-9420).

# Pedaling with Overseas Peddlers

**S**igning up overseas distributors at trade shows can be painless. Some distributors will even pay you in advance. But, seller beware: Those easy orders can lead to major obstacles down the road.

Scott Montgomery, marketing chief at Cannondale, a Bethel, Conn., bike manufacturer, recalls his struggle to control distribution when he started Cannondale Europe, in 1989. Sales raced to $1.5 million the first year, but margins slipped. The same distributors that placed large orders and paid with letters of credit also resorted to discounting. "When your products are being dumped," says Montgomery, "you lose control of your pricing and positioning."

To reestablish his authority, he **bought out the contracts of his European distributors and agents** in 1992, for an "embarrassingly expensive price"—about 5% of the reps' annual commissions. Says a wiser Montgomery: "You can do okay with agents and distributors if you protect yourself. You should overstate that you're signing a short-term agreement, otherwise you may still have to pay. It's not like in the United States."

Montgomery has since set up a sales force, opened an office in the Netherlands, and built warehouse space. Cannondale Europe's annual sales are now pedaling along at $60 million.

# V

"A customer's not a customer
until he's a repeat customer."

**SAM WALTON**
founder, Wal-Mart,
Bentonville, Ark.

**144**

**IDEA**

# Sell Less, Gain More

**E**veryone knows about upselling to generate more revenues per customer, but **downselling a customer** can be an equally effective sales strategy in the long run. Kristine Bierman, owner of Colt Safety Products, an industrial-safety products distributor based in St. Louis, hit upon this counterintuitive approach while trying to build customer loyalty.

"Some customers were ordering excessive numbers of safety glasses and gloves because workers weren't properly trained to take care of them," explains Bierman. "So, I offered to train their employees to use the safety equipment. As a result, their orders dropped from 40 gloves a month to four." The loss of sales didn't hurt at all because it resulted in tremendous word-of-mouth advertising, which brings in more sales. "It helps distinguish us from the pack of volume-oriented commodity competitors out there," says Bierman, whose downselling strategy has helped grow her company to $1.7 million in sales.

**IDEA**

# Playing Matchmaker

**W**hen you can't supply what customers or clients need, **send them to another supplier** instead of playing dumb. Even if it's a competitor, giving guidance will improve your standing in the long run.

Frank Sennett, owner and president of General Machine, in Windham, Maine, runs a shop that makes parts for electronics manufacturers. His customers sometimes need parts he can't make or can't price competitively. So he shares his industry expertise and network of contacts. Although he might be turning down short-term business, he says it helps secure long-term advantages for General Machine.

"Helping our customers gives us a team-member image," he explains. "If they're going to seek this information anyway, our position only gets better if we are helpful, honest, and not threatened by their request." Acting like a partner encourages customers to communicate openly, too— and that's the payoff. "We're better able to assess their needs and make adjustments to our service early to match changes in their operations," Sennett says. Two regular customers now include him in their new-product planning as the plastic-parts expert. "I get in on the ground level on new projects," he says, "so I can get the cream-of-the-crop jobs."

**146**

IDEA

# Unbuttoned by Design

Usually, it's not a product's basic design that turns a customer off, it's a nagging detail. To find out what those little bugs are, executives at Dia, a manufacturer of hand-knit women's sweaters in Vergennes, Vt., **talk with customers at trunk shows in boutiques**.

Although customers said that they loved the sweaters, they frequently reported that the unique buttons, which they originally found so charming, were troublesome: Every time a sweater needed dry cleaning, the buttons would have to be cut off and resewn on afterward; otherwise, they would be damaged. CEO John Leehman figured that if a few loyal fans of Dia sweaters were mentioning this drawback, more prospects probably weren't reordering because of the inconvenience.

So to increase repeat sales, the company improved the design of the product. Now the buttons are made to attach like cufflinks, which can be easily removed for dry cleaning. The new process of attaching the buttons costs no more than sewing them on. "The change has actually speeded up production and given us a sales edge against our competitors," says Leehman. In 1997, the company posted more than $4 million in revenues.

**147**

**IDEA**

# Never Complain, Always Explain

**W**hen customers get sticker shock, they're likely to grill you: What is it about this product that makes it cost so much? If you're using desktop publishing technology, they may expect something for nothing because it looks so easy. Marketing and communications firms, in particular, are directly threatened by do-it-yourself technology.

Rather than talk until she was blue in the face about how much work still goes into a project despite the miraculous software, Carol Lasky, owner of Cahoots!, a small, Boston-based marketing-communications firm, depends upon **trade journal articles to give customers the big picture**.

"We educate customers about how our field has changed as a result of electronic publishing," says Lasky. "For example, I faxed one customer an article on ownership rights of electronic files. If that customer asks for a copy of a file and I say there will be a fee for it, he won't be surprised. Enlightened customers understand where we are coming from and are less likely to make unreasonable demands upon us. With fewer disappointments, customers are more satisfied overall."

# 148
**IDEA**

# Here's How We Make Magic

**A**t the onset of a relationship with a new customer, everyone has great expectations. Once work begins, making sure that the customer's expectations don't disintegrate into disappointments is one of a company owner's key responsibilities. After all, high customer-satisfaction ratings are vital to increasing repeat sales—one of the most inexpensive ways for a company to grow revenues.

Sealund Associates, a publisher of technical manuals in Clearwater, Fla., meets customers' expectations by **teaching them the tricks of its trade**. "We take the time to teach customers professional proofreading and copy-editing marks to use when correcting drafts, so that their changes can be incorporated with a minimum of fuss," explains Barbara Sealund, founder. "We fax them documents that they must mark up. We won't let them tell us what they want changed over the telephone, because that leaves too much room for misunderstandings." Sealund Associates must be doing something right by eliminating potential hassles—in 1997, repeat business comprised 90% of sales.

# 149
## IDEA

# Tactful Undertaking

**C**ompanies that need to gather sensitive, personal information from customers face a unique set of challenges—just ask any home health care worker, attorney, retirement or life insurance sales rep, or anyone offering financial, day care, rehab, or handicap services. So when the Federal Trade Commission ordered funeral directors to adopt realistic pricing structures, to provide itemized price lists, and to analyze costs, a certain amount of business savvy and attention to the bottom line became necessary to compete. However, the tools that other companies use to streamline operations and improve service can backfire in the "deathcare" industry, where a strategically placed box of tissues can mean more than a state-of-the-art ordering system.

John McDonough, owner of McDonough Funeral Home, in Lowell, Mass., found that the best strategy for introducing technology into the business—while maintaining the warm human presence that customers expect—was to deploy the computer as transparently as possible. McDonough casually uses a Macintosh Powerbook to record customers' answers to the dozens of questions he asks to plan a funeral. The bereaved are often more curious than upset to find him using a laptop to take their information—they even lean over to see what he is doing. In response, he **attaches a remote monitor to his laptop so that customers can watch as he fills in the forms**. As a result of this tactic, McDonough saves time and makes fewer errors. Details, such as the need for extra limos, no longer slip between the cracks—and as any funeral director knows, getting the details right means providing customers with quality care.

# Flooring the Customer

**S**hop-floor employees closest to production are often best qualified to understand customers' needs. Tom Jagemann, president and CEO of Jagemann Stamping, a family-owned tool-and-die shop in Manitowoc, Wis., **makes his line employees an integral part of the sales team**. Whenever a problem arises, a small group of line workers is sent out with either a salesperson or an engineer to investigate at the customer's site.

Taking production workers on-site shows customers how much they get for their money, says Jagemann. "It also helps raise employees' level of commitment to the customer, because they see how the product is ultimately used and have a sense of the conditions that the user has to deal with."

Jagemann Stamping tries to avoid making a distinction between labor and management, a culture that has earned the company lifetime customers. Since 1993, it has lost only 1 of the top 25 accounts that make up 80% of its business—and then, with a bit of hard work, it managed to woo the same client back. The 52-year-old company's 1997 revenues came to $30 million.

## Line-Item Veto

It's one thing to adopt a strategy calling for better customer service. It's another to devise a mechanism that forces employees to pay attention when your company isn't meeting the standards that customers expect. Granite Rock, a heavy-engineering contractor and concrete, asphalt, and gravel producer based in Watsonville, Calif., underscores its ambitious mission statement with gutsy practices like its dramatic "short pay" policy. Printed on the back of every Granite Rock invoice is the following: "If you're not satisfied with something, don't pay us for it. Simply scratch out the related line item and send your check for the remaining balance."

**Inviting dissatisfied customers to pay less than the amount on the invoice** is certain to make people take notice. It's concrete. It's measurable. And pretty soon, the entire company—from sales staff to mixer-truck drivers—is trying to perform so well that it won't happen.

**152**
**IDEA**

# Basket Case

"**O**rdering a gift basket is the type of thing people do after they've had a long day," says Cynthia Mantzoukas, owner and manager of The Proper Basket, in Lynn, Mass., a company that designs and delivers specialty gift baskets for corporate clients. While she couldn't personally take phone calls 24 hours a day, Mantzoukas didn't want to lose any customers. So, she decided to **catch their orders with a fax machine after hours**.

Mantzoukas designed a one-page fax order form and mailed it with a brochure to all her customers. Orders came in right away, from all over. "A client who was traveling in Seattle met a hot prospect in a hotel and faxed me an order to send a basket there," she recalls. Now, regular customers who might be working late can catch up on thank-yous during those quiet working hours. Orders that are waiting for Mantzoukas when she opens in the morning are delivered that day.

Mantzoukas keeps the program pumped by including a fax form with invoices and by mailing them to first-time callers, along with a brochure. Faxes account for 10% of all orders.

**153**
**IDEA**

## Recipe for Success

It's important to keep a database of your customers. It's important to send personalized cards and appropriate gifts in the hope of more sales. But it's even better to **remember customers' needs and send them useful information**.

Pam Kadlec, co-owner of P.K. Whiskers Wildlife Art & Taxidermy Studio, in Starke, Fla., devotes considerable energy to building value-added customer relationships. She keeps customers' names and addresses in a database, along with notes about their last hunting trophy, and sends them hard-to-find recipes: hearty venison dishes for deer hunters, sophisticated duck à l'orange for duck shooters. "A lot of people find a taxidermist by word of mouth," she explains, "not through newspaper ads. So I try to keep my good customers happy." And it's hard to forget a service provider who helps you wow your dinner guests twice—with what's on the table as well as what's on the wall.

**154**

IDEA

# Anniversary Waltz

**J**ust a little reminder can boost your sales while keeping your customers in the good graces of their mothers-in-law. Clifford's Flowers, in Quincy, Mass., **uses sales records to generate letters reminding past customers to order again** for upcoming birthdays or anniversaries. This may sound obvious, but it's effective. James Clifford, owner of the $5-million florist, has found that 75% to 85% of customers who get the letter reorder.

While he may be playing on his customers' guilt—now they *have* to send flowers to Great-aunt Gertrude—or whether they are enticed by the specials he offers in the letters, Clifford has not only dramatically boosted sales but has also probably saved a few marriages and friendships. He is amazed by the success of this simple tactic. "I never dreamed that three out of four customers would say, 'Yes, send my mother roses again,'" he says. But his combination of reminder and convenience makes it easy for past customers to become repeat customers, thereby generating new sales.

# 155
## IDEA

# Virtual Roundtable

**J**anice Gjertsen, director of marketing and business development for Digital City, a Manhattan division of America Online, believes strongly in testing new programs. But when she wanted to gauge reaction to her company's Web site, an events guide to the city, she added a twist to the traditional roundtable by **taking her focus group online**.

She contacted Cyber Dialogue, a company also located in New York City that specializes in online database marketing and market research. Cyber Dialogue drew from its database of some 12,000 people for the focus group, provided the moderator, and superimposed the focus group onto a chat room at Digital City's "Total New York" Web site. Gjertsen looked on from her desktop computer and used software that let her interact with the moderator without the focus group knowing.

The results surprised her. "People were more honest online than they were in our traditional groups," she says. At $3,000, an online focus group cost one-third that of a traditional group. It yielded quick results, too: Gjertsen received a full report in a day, instead of the usual four weeks.

**156**

**IDEA**

## Postcards for the Edge

**M**any small companies just don't have enough news to fill a newsletter, let alone time to produce one. Instead, Duane Jones of Storm Products, an electronics manufacturer in Phoenix, sends out 500 "newscards" a month. He pays a freelance writer $100 per "issue" and a printer $10 per 100 copies. Using postcards saves him 12¢ a piece on postage. **Sending customers a mini-mailer** is a good way to keep in contact and provide them with useful tidbit information. For companies that need to use graphic imagery on their postcards, a copying process called Docutech can provide extremely high-quality graphics, while only raising the cost of a card to about 30¢ each. "It's a lot of bang for the buck," says Jones, who has seen a number of his mailers pinned to customers' walls.

# Backup for the Band

One way to eliminate time-consuming follow-up with prospects is to follow through immediately when you meet them. This becomes critically important at trade shows, where sales leads and even orders can easily get lost in a wave of business at a company's booth. Peavey Electronics, in Meridian, Miss., makes sure its sales representatives can keep up with the many dealers who visit its booth at the National Association of Music Merchants' mammoth annual trade show in Anaheim, Calif. The guitar and audio electronics manufacturer brings along **one sales support staffer for every two sales reps to process orders on the spot**. Because many dealers buy nearly half a year's worth of inventory at one show, it's imperative that Peavey be prepared to keep up with business during those critical four days. Jere Hess, the company's spokesperson, says that the cost of being overstaffed far outweighs the risk of being understaffed and losing orders in the expo frenzy.

**158**

IDEA

# Dress Rehearsal

**A** service guarantee promising "satisfaction or your money back" can be a powerful sales tool—if you have the systems in place to make good on your word. Before going public with its written guarantee, CPS Direct, a provider of direct-marketing services in Woburn, Mass., began a **yearlong dress rehearsal of its guarantee program** within the 170-employee company.

"Many mistakes happen because procedures aren't defined," says Jim Hackett, former vice-president of sales. Salespeople would discuss ideas for direct-mail pieces with clients, scribble down the details, and give them to account managers for production. CPS couldn't pinpoint how many little mistakes originated in that information hand-off until it launched an internal service guarantee consisting of:

❧ *The promise.* It could be specific ("I will deliver X service by X date") or sweeping (the CPS salespeople pledged to give account managers all the information they needed to do their jobs).

❧ *The payout.* If a salesperson delivers inaccurate or incomplete specifications, for example, the account managers choose the "payment": treat me to lunch, do the data-entry work for the job yourself, or sing a song of my choice at the next sales meeting.

❧ *The invocation procedure.* Activating the internal guarantee should be easy; CPS employees deliver a simple invocation form to the person who erred.

Among the payoffs of the program: A standard one-page "job-launch form" was created for salespeople to use to record crucial details, which reduced the number of order entries with errors from 50% to 10%. And "those errors are real minutiae," says Hackett.

# Focus, Baby, Focus

**F**ocus groups are a great way to get closer to your customers—to solidify your relationship with current customers and to forge relationships with new ones. They can evaluate your company's success and determine a path for the future. And they'll tell you what customers are looking for and how you can better provide it. You don't even need to hire a marketing firm to put together a suitable collection of consumers. You can **use local newspapers to find potential focus-group participants**.

When Karen Scott of Lake Bluff, Ill., got started in the mail-order baby-products business, she put together her own focus group by clipping 250 birth announcements from the local paper, then contacting the new moms. She sent them surveys and conducted phone interviews, asking what products young mothers sought. In response to their comments, Scott added more travel products to her consumer catalog, "One Step Ahead," which allows customers to order directly from her company, Chelsea & Scott. In 1998, travel products are still top sellers at the $35-million business.

**160**
IDEA

# Field Marshals

The best folks to turn to for marketing advice may be the independent salespeople who represent your company. Not only are they most familiar with your product, they have firsthand experience of its reception in the marketplace.

Instead of plugging his products at meetings with his manufacturers' reps, Ed Muldoon, owner of Bivar, a $10-million electronics manufacturer in Irvine, Calif., tries to benefit from his reps' field experience. Prior to a recent two-day Bivar conference in Chicago, five longtime Bivar salespeople **sent out surveys to fellow representatives, asking for input on product ideas and market analysis**. At the conference, the group came up with responses and critiqued Bivar's sales-and-service support. Then the participants created a plan to put their ideas to work. Though the meeting was not cheap for Bivar, Muldoon claims it was worth it: Feedback was applied immediately, and the ideas will result in new products and marketing strategies.

"When you hire salespeople, you're not just choosing employees. You're also choosing customers. Like it or not, your salespeople are going to play a major role in determining the types of customers you have and the kinds of relationships you have with them."

**NORM BRODSKY**
founder and CEO, CitiStorage,
Brooklyn, N.Y.

**161**
**IDEA**

# Whose Foot's in the Door?

If you are trying to break into a new geographic area, you can show up cold on potential customers' doorsteps. Or you can contact a manufacturer of complementary products with significant distribution in that region and ask which sales reps they use. Buyers tend to trust people with whom they've done business in the past. And while not everyone will share a talented rep, some manufacturers will happily pass along names.

Tony Prisco, owner of GI Apparel, a $20-million company in Farmingdale, N.J., routinely **turns to other companies for help finding top-notch reps** to sell his novelty T-shirt line. "They know who the good reps are," says Prisco. "They've already done your job for you." If he's trying to get into a particular store, Prisco contacts the buyers and asks them to recommend a rep. Buyers like to work with only a limited number of vendors, but they sometimes buy from Prisco if he can go through someone they already deal with.

# 162
**IDEA**

## College Draft

**P**atrick Kelly, CEO of PSS/World Medical, in Jacksonville, Fla., was having trouble finding experienced salespeople for his rapidly growing company. Competitors were fighting hard to keep their best people, and if he lured one away, the ex-employer would likely slap PSS with a lawsuit. Previously, Kelly had good luck hiring recent college graduates, so he decided to pursue that strategy with a vengeance.

Kelly and his two partners, both experienced medical-products sales reps, began **visiting local colleges on Career Day**. Over time, they refined the profile of their ideal sales candidate. Experience didn't matter. Attitude and behavior did.

The strategy has paid off in a number of ways. Recent grads are mobile, so the company rarely has trouble finding salespeople for a new facility. They don't mind starting with low pay and earning their advancement. Most of all, newbies can be fired up. The company communicates a "reward for hard work" message by rigorously promoting from within, regardless of age or seniority—and by not batting an eyelash when youthful high achievers earn outrageous sums of money. Today, all of PSS's regional vice-presidents are homegrown.

# 163
### IDEA

• BUILDING YOUR SALES FORCE •

## Never Too Late to Sell

**W**hen Jo Anne Schiller lost her job in publishing, she rejected retirement to start her own company, Everyday Learning, which develops a core curriculum in math for elementary schools. Naturally enough, she **recruited her first sales reps from the ranks of the newly retired**.

Schiller, 60, first hired a salesperson she knew from her old job, who tapped fellow retired reps and subsequently headed sales. The reps, aged 55 to 65, helped jump-start sales in nine regions in which they'd been working for years, including Illinois, New York, and Texas. They agreed to work on commission, since they had retired with pensions or accepted early retirement packages. "They could afford to take the time to help us build this up," says Schiller, president and CEO.

The marketing and customer-service managers were also plucked from retirement and given equity in the Chicago company. With about 120 employees, Everyday Learning is in the black—and on the blackboards in 100,000 classrooms.

# 164
## IDEA

## Once Upon a Mattress

**W**ould you hire someone with no retail management experience to run your store? Select Comfort, a Minneapolis manufacturer of high-quality air mattresses, does. Before entering a new retail market, the company sends recruitment postcards to "Comfort Club" members—customers who have spent at least $1,200 on its innovative "sleep system." "We knew that if we had converts to what we were doing, we could train them in the selling process," says Mark de Naray, board member and former CEO.

Select Comfort's **satisfied customers make effective salespeople**. Karen McFarland was initially skeptical of the company's claims—her husband, who suffers from a degenerative spinal ailment, ordered his mattress in secret using a neighbor's phone because she thought it was a gimmick. Now she believes the bed saved her husband from surgery. McFarland's enthusiasm for the product persuaded area sales manager Tim Brasfield to hire her to manage the Cary, N.C., store. He was glad he did: Her store exceeded its sales goals for 11 of 12 months, earning it three top-performance rankings.

# 165
### IDEA

# Temporary Solution

**B**eating a competitor to market with a new product really mattered to Bob Trussell of Tempur-Pedic, a six-year-old importer and distributor in Lexington, Ky. He wanted to get his orthopedic mattresses into 10 regional markets in six months, but he couldn't afford to get bogged down hiring a sales force. Instead, the company turned to Sales Staffers International, in Danvers, Mass., for transitional outsourcing help.

"It's not cheap, but it's a lot faster," says Trussell. He paid Sales Staffers $275 an hour to set up videoconferencing with about 75 remotely located candidates, a $12.50 base hourly rate for the reps plus a 50% to 60% surcharge that went to the agency, and a $2,000 release fee that Tempur-Pedic paid to retain certain salespeople after a 90-day period. That was still 20% less, Trussell believes, than it would have cost him to employ full-time personnel dedicated to recruiting. Although the reps were paid by the outsourcing company, Trussell set the pay rate and created the goals. When a rep wasn't working out, Sales Staffers would send a replacement, saving Trussell the hassle and costs.

Trussell was satisfied with the results. "Although it's a lot of cash up front, **outsourcing the sales staffing** makes sense when you're small and growing." With $30 million in 1997 revenues, Tempur-Pedic now boasts its own sales staff of 15, 1 of whom came from the outsourcing service.

# 166
## IDEA

• BUILDING YOUR SALES FORCE •

# Flowering Power

**P**enny and Frank Burkard, of Burkard Nurseries, in Pasadena, Calif., nurture sales as carefully as they tend their perennials, roses, and Japanese maple saplings. In 1992, like many retailers, they depended on a handful of full-time employees. "We discovered our sales staff was stale," says Penny Burkard. "They didn't communicate a passion for gardening to our customers." To solve the problem, the Burkards decided to **use a larger pool of talented and enthusiastic part-timers**.

The benefits that the Burkards derive from this strategy far outweigh the scheduling headaches of working with 30 part-timers. "They are wonderful employees; I'll take them when I can get them," says Burkard. If someone calls in sick, it's much easier to find a replacement. The store isn't left short-handed, and employees can work out schedule changes among themselves to accommodate their personal needs. The strategy also allows the nursery to hire horticultural students. They can infect customers with their enthusiasm and are better able to answer a serious collector's questions than a less educated but more available person. The downside? Employees must clean up unfinished projects when they leave.

One student has taken on the project of cataloguing the nursery's formidable collection of more than 600 varieties of roses and thousands of perennials, so that plants can be labeled. "You can't get that kind of dedication from someone who is just showing up for a paycheck," says Burkard. "Now we'll have another sales tool to help customers choose their plants." Freshening up the staff has helped keep sales growing by about 20% annually since 1992; they reached nearly $2 million in 1997.

# Picking Sales Hotshots

**I**f independent sales agents are the lifeblood of your business, you know that good producers are hard to find and even harder to hold onto. About 80% of sales agents in the insurance industry, for example, don't even make it through the first year.

So to recruit good producers, Jim Zacha CLU, vice-president and co-owner of K&J Marketing Concepts, in New Smyrna Beach, Fla., beats the odds by **using referrals and interviewing prospects on a one-on-one basis**. K&J is a $500,000 independent marketing firm that sells insurance products for LifeUSA through a distribution network comprised of more than 800 independent agents. K&J earns anywhere from 1% to 20% on all products its producers sell. Considering that a good producer can generate as many as 10 contracts worth $110,000 to $130,000 a month, the importance of recruiting good producers is not lost on K&J.

Zacha's method of recruiting reps runs counter to that of the insurance industry, which typically recruits by direct mail and telemarketing. However, this results in a high turnover rate and low success ratio. K&J, on the other hand, boasts a low producer turnover rate and growth of more than 20% a year.

Zacha's formula for picking winners? "If someone has been in the business for more than five years, chances are he or she will succeed. If their marketing efforts can use our products, we have a good fit."

**IDEA**

# Star Bright, Not Quite Right

**D**o you have a sales representative who is driven, dauntless, and phenomenally productive—by all measures, a star? If so, are the competitive friction with coworkers and thirst for autonomy and recognition worth the sales and profits that person generates? You may well be wondering how to drag that superstar down to earth.

Marie Clapper, president and publisher of Clapper Communications Cos., a $12-million magazine publisher in Des Plaines, Ill., says that spending 22 years supervising 60 employees has taught her to **weed out recruits who won't fit into the company's culture**—which is resolutely open and team-spirited. One giveaway is a candidate's discomfort with a "no locked doors" policy. Anybody who feels strongly about having a closed office isn't likely to fit in at a place that values team players.

Another tactic for ferreting out prima donnas during interviews is to ask for examples of success as a member of a team. If the applicant can't think of a good answer or responds instead with a strong individual achievement, you may want to hire someone else.

# 169
## IDEA

# Handwritten Invitation

In Europe, graphology is widely used by large corporations to detect personality traits as varied as ego drive and risk aversion. Within the United States, it's the risk-taking entrepreneurs who **use handwriting analysis to identify the best candidates for sales jobs**. Tom Payette, for one, hires a graphologist to help him ferret out winners for his $30-million Jaguar and Suzuki dealership in Louisville, Ky. He claims the technique has significantly reduced his annual sales-force turnover rate, which at 36% is nearly half the industry average.

Payette didn't always feel that way. "Like most people, I thought handwriting analysis was a bunch of hocus-pocus," he recalls. Then Iris Hatfield, president of HuVista International, changed his mind after her incisive analysis of his own personality.

Hatfield, whose graphology business has more than 300 clients nationwide, devised "success profiles" for Payette's salespeople, based on a composite of the handwriting characteristics of the top performers. Payette invites job applicants to submit to the graphology test as a second or third screen, after reviewing résumés and holding initial interviews.

"I may develop a gut feeling about someone, but handwriting analysis gives me a standard by which to measure the person," observes Payette. It also enables him to spot undesirable qualities, such as excessive sensitivity to criticism. The auto dealer sends samples to HuVista; for $45 he gets back a "Quick-Screen Analysis"—one page on the writer's key traits, with a letter grade. If Payette questions something in the summary, he'll occasionally buy the full 12-page, $250 report on the candidate.

# 170
**IDEA**

# Triple-Scoop Sellers

**S**uper-premium ice-cream stores, once a safe niche, have become almost as easy to find as espresso shops. So Amy Miller needed a new recipe to differentiate Amy's Ice Creams, her seven-store chain in Austin, San Antonio, and Houston. To get customers inside, she decided to stage promotions on a regular basis—impromptu musical comedies, costumes and jokes, and frivolous contests. She wasn't just selling ice cream, she was selling an experience. To create that experience, she had to get the right employees and get them to behave the right way. And because their behavior needed to be inventive, unflagging, and self-initiated, they had to know what the right way was without being told.

To find those super-premium people, Amy's Ice Creams **gives job applicants a plain white paper bag with instructions to do anything they want with it** and bring it back in a week. Those who just jot down a phone number will find that Amy's isn't really for them. But anyone who can make something unusual from a white paper bag tends to be an amusing person who can fit in and promote the product. Applicants have turned bags into a giant cone supporting the earth, board games, works of art, and elaborate parodies ("The Amysburg Address"). One who went on to become a manager handed out $5 gift certificates to customers willing to do their best animal impression. The exercise reminds would-be scoopers that creativity, not just ice cream, is what their boss really puts a premium on, and it helped the company bring in $2.2 million in 1997.

**IDEA**

# Sounding Out Candidates

**W**hen Chuck Surack, president of Sweetwater Sound, in Fort Wayne, Ind., hires telephone salespeople, he runs help-wanted ads in newspapers **listing only the position and a telephone number**. Callers get a recording that introduces Surack's $40-million musical-equipment company and gives them five minutes to explain why they should be hired. Any caller who provides a good "audio résumé" is asked to submit a written one.

"It's amazing, the number of people who are uncomfortable on the phone," observes Surack. And obviously, good salespeople have to know how to beam their smile through a telephone wire.

# 172
**IDEA**

## Road-Show Auditions

**A**t Microtraining Plus, a Macintosh-training company in Norwalk, Conn., prospective trainers and salespeople need more than good interviewing skills and glowing references. "We're hiring people for their ability to get up in front of six people they don't know and present material," says CEO David Knise. Like an increasing number of CEOs, he **requires job applicants to demonstrate their skills in a live performance**.

Candidates give Microtraining's eight-member staff an hour-long presentation on any topic other than computers. "Because we're computer people, we'd focus too much on whether what [applicants] say is right or wrong, instead of on their ability to teach," explains Knise. Among others, reports on the solar system and the instruments in an orchestra got thumbs up; attempts to teach Italian, in-line skating, and math were deemed unsuccessful. "We see how applicants organize their thoughts, whether they've given themselves enough time to cover the material, and whether they have overall command of the classroom," says Knise. He also notes whether candidates appear to be focusing on him during their talks (more confident people don't play to him as much) and how they react to disruptive participants.

REAL
WORLD

"The acid test for hiring?
Ask yourself, How would you
feel having this same person
working for your competition
instead of for you?"

**HARVEY MACKAY**
chairman and CEO, Mackay Envelope Corp.,
Minneapolis, and author of *Swim with the Sharks Without
Being Eaten Alive* (William Morrow)

## Avoid Party Animals

**S**elling to governments can take a notoriously long time. In desperation, many companies succumb to the charms of so-called political consultants, who promise access to top government officials in exchange for a fee or retainer. However, beware of consultants who are tied too closely to politicians in office. Once a government changes after an election, you and the consultant may be ousted along with other politically appointed employees and contractors.

Instead, Mike Davis, CEO of The VINE Co., a Louisville firm that sells automated victim-notification systems to county and state governments, **hires salespeople who thrive on long-term sales development**. He looks for successful, extremely organized sales managers who are good at staying on top of 40 projects and inching them along through each step necessary to complete each sale. "They know they aren't going to close a deal in the first meeting or come back with a contract in a month, and they are okay with that," notes Davis.

# Sizing Up First-String Sales Pros

**T**ony Razzano, chief scout for the San Francisco 49ers in the 1980s, watched prospective players perform in 200 plays. That allowed him to spot quarterback legend Joe Montana, a third-round draft pick. Of course, you'll rarely see 200 moves by a job applicant, but you can check out 20 or so—before, during, and after an interview. Dr. Pierre Mornell, a hiring consultant in Marin County, Calif., who wrote *Hiring Smart: How to Predict Winners and Losers in the Incredibly Expensive People-Reading Game* (Ten Speed Press, 1998, $24.95), suggests these **tactics to see a candidate in action**:

&. *Read résumés in teams.* Teams are more apt to spot inconsistencies and formulate an opinion of what's truly important to the company as a whole. One member of a team may see a candidate's ability to take risks as a negative and another may view it as a positive. A third may spot a gap in a candidate's job history.

&. *Ask all your questions at once.* Performance depends on the candidate, not on selling yourself and the organization. This strategy also directly confronts the most common problem in an interview: talking too much. Finally, it forces an interviewer to listen. Settle back and watch the applicant's behavior while listening to him or her.

# 175
**IDEA**

# Target Hiring

**A**ttracting seasoned salespeople was always a challenge for Tony Chachere's Creole Food, a $12-million manufacturer in Opelousas, La. The company's remote location was only part of the problem. After taking a sales-management course, sales vice-president Mona Campbell realized that she needed **to improve her interviewing techniques**.

First, she audited her own sales strengths. "I had to figure out my motivations before I could write interview questions that would unlock the candidate's motivations," says Campbell. "It hit me that I needed to focus on what I do best—find new business."

Her next search—for someone to maintain accounts—was different, and her ad, which directed replies to a bigger city's post office, attracted 160 applicants. Twelve made the cut, and Campbell selected Nanette Fisher, a gifted manager of retail accounts, because she had suggested great ways to support Campbell's opening of new territories.

At Fisher's previous employer, L'Oréal, she had developed a network of part-time employees who visited stores and built relationships. "She spelled out how she could do the same for us," says Campbell. "She knew how to recruit reps, train them, and track their progress."

# 176
### IDEA

## Glued to the Screen

**S**alespeople at Select Comfort, a Minneapolis manufacturer of high-quality air mattresses, sharpen their skills by going to the movies. In addition to being trained by area managers, new hires at Select Comfort's retail stores complete a **video training program** on the company's selling method, called Desire Fulfillment Selling. They also get a two-day orientation at the University of Select Comfort, an internal training facility that also offers ongoing skills courses.

Videos keep salespeople up to date on ever-changing company activities, too. A monthly video called *Talking Select* keeps all employees abreast of new production techniques, plans for expansion, the results of market research, or other companywide issues.

So rather than sending out a newsletter that employees may not read, offer them something both creative and enjoyable that you can be sure they'll watch—on company time.

**IDEA**

# To Train Is to Gain

**N**o sooner would a salesperson slip inside Tom Patrevito's office than the same tedious dialogue would begin. Each of his sales reps had a customer who needed a special break on pricing, and the demands were accompanied by the same threat: Meet this price, or we talk to one of your dozens of competitors. Patrevito's company, Booklet Binding, in Broadview, Ill., was feeling the squeeze on its margins as profits stayed put even when sales climbed.

If management doesn't take a proactive role in establishing a strategy for the sales staff, a company like Booklet Binding can't possibly safeguard its profitability. Instead of resorting to layoffs and price cuts, there's a third option often overlooked by managers: instituting **a sales training program led by a highly qualified consultant**. That's the high road Booklet Binding, a graphic arts finishing and direct mail production house, took.

Topics at its 20-week program, held over the course of 10 months, include precall planning, preparing a presentation, following up, selling value, and coping with objections to price. When the class graduates, salespeople are prepared to teach customers how to make their own businesses more profitable—differentiating Booklet Binding from other binderies.

Initially, Patrevito reports, there were plenty of objections to the program. But once he pointed out how it could enrich individuals and the company, employees were more willing to learn new ways to sell. In 1994, the company rendered fewer than 1,500 quotes a month. That number is up to 2,500 in 1998, and more quotes are turning into jobs. With sales of $22 million, the company is posting pretax margins roughly twice what they were prior to the sales training program.

# 178
**IDEA**

# Method Acting

**R**eally successful telephone selling involves much more than an auto-dialer and a well-written script. Chuck Surack, whose company sells its audio equipment largely by phone, has been polishing the art of telephone selling since he started Sweetwater Sound, in Fort Wayne, Ind., with his wife in 1979. "We constantly work to perfect the art of controlled conversation," says Surack.

To rehearse their act, Sweetwater Sound's 40 **phone salespeople attend thrice-weekly training classes** led by the president and vice-president of sales, as well as top sales reps. Newcomers attend for eight hours; more experienced reps go for four. Surack says the program not only educates the sales staff and improves its rap, it also helps prevent burnout on the job. The company's turnover rate is less than 2%.

Half the teaching time is devoted to role-playing. The other half is spent fine-tuning the dialogue and other selling basics, as well as reviewing new products. "Employees contribute botched sales calls to the class to use as examples," Surack says. "Role-playing really helps people remember what is being taught. Besides, everybody gets a chuckle out of it." Sessions are videotaped so that employees can make up the ones they miss and show recruits on their first anniversary how much they've improved since their first days at work.

Surack doesn't regret any sales lost because employees were attending training sessions. The company's emphasis on training is a key to its success: Selling highly technical equipment that costs thousands of dollars, Sweetwater Sound chalked up more than $31 million in sales last year—with no face-to-face meetings.

# 179
## IDEA

## Rallying Overseas Reps

**W**hen a dispersed overseas sales force fails to live up to expectations, what can you do to bring sales back in line? Restek, which does business in more than 50 countries, gathered its far-flung reps for three days of training at company headquarters in Bellefonte, Pa.

Restek, a manufacturer of chromatography supplies, realized that its overseas business was far below expectations—only 10% of its $10.5 million in sales instead of an anticipated 25%, so the company faced up to a critical oversight. It was not **giving enough direction to its foreign distributors**. A question-and-answer session with the reps revealed that what they needed most was help in selling to secondary markets. So Restek prepared a grid matching market niches with applications for its supplies, and it intensified hands-on product training. The company also agreed to pay more attention to the reps' small, but important, requests (e.g., "Don't send 'free' demo packages, because customs will assign them a value.").

Sessions on marketing elicited debates on the merits of direct mail in small markets compared to larger territories. Some reps ran marketing mini-tutorials: The Italian distributor addressed how to best translate Restek product literature, and a U.S. rep, newly hired from the competition, analyzed rival companies' selling techniques.

Although it would have been cheaper (the total bill came to about $50,000) for Restek to have held the training session during a major trade show in Europe, the U.S. event allowed the reps to meet the whole Restek organization. Within a year of the gathering, the company had achieved its original goal: Overseas business accounted for 25% of sales.

# One a Day Keeps Skills in Play

**W**hether your salespeople are rookies or veterans, it pays for them to assess their selling skills periodically. Could they use a few pointers (or reminders) on how to get past customer resistance? How about managing sales territories?

*The Idea-a-Day Guide to Super Selling and Customer Service*, by Tony Alessandra, Gary Couture, and Gregg Baron (Dartnell, 800-621-5463, 1992, $21.50) serves as a convenient **refresher course for salespeople at all levels**, including CEOs. Each of the book's 15 sections addresses a specific sales skill, from setting goals to building customer satisfaction. The ideas are accompanied by more than 100 work sheets. There are eight work sheets, for example, on analyzing your accounts, and seven on identifying lucrative prospects.

"The book's very useful in prodding old-time salespeople into rethinking their processes and getting new salespeople on track," says Mike McDoniels, CEO of MJ Altman, a $2.2-million collection and billing agency in Ocala, Fla. McDoniels has three salespeople and spends about 25% of his own time on sales and marketing. He has used *Idea-a-Day* in teaching a sales course for his industry association and has found the sections on knowing your products, managing time, and setting goals particularly valuable.

# Curtain Going Up

**P**resentations are performances. The best way to prepare for a performance is to rehearse. So, why not borrow a technique from the theater and **hold dress rehearsals for sales presentations**?

HMC Group, a $16-million architectural-design business in Ontario, Calif., does exactly that—even providing an audience for its budding stars. The head of marketing acts as the director, leading the salespeople as they run through their presentations. Senior staff members act as customers and ask tough questions culled from past client meetings. The scenario is made as realistic as possible, and it gives presenters a chance to polish their acts with the support and feedback of their colleagues.

Afterward, the audience, now playing the role of *New York Times* drama columnists, critiques the cast and gives advice on script revision. "They judge more harshly than a client ever would," says CEO Robert Kain. Well-rehearsed presenters are then prepared for the worst, and they usually end up giving their best.

# 182
## IDEA

# Higher Education

**S**alespeople who work their way up the chain of command at a customer's company may have to field increasingly harder questions about specific capabilities. "We said we were experts, but we weren't," admits Tom Patrevito, co-owner of Booklet Binding, in Broadview, Ill. His solution: **Have salespeople give team presentations in front of peers and in-house experts**. Salespeople at Booklet Binding teamed up and spent eight weeks becoming experts in a topic area—saddle stitching, perfect binding, mailing, cutting, customer service, scheduling, estimating, and so on—then prepared a two- to three-hour presentation, complete with handouts.

One team created a takeoff on *Reader's Digest*, teaching about customer service under such familiar headings as "Laughter, the Best Medicine" and "Points to Ponder." A group studying pricing came up with a Jeopardy-style game. The program, which lasted over the course of a year, helped bring the sales representatives—who work on individual commission—together with other employees in the company. In addition, several sales reps have been invited to customers' sites to lecture on such topics as label personalization and postage tactics.

**183**

IDEA

# Into the Wild Blue Yonder

**T**ackling emerging markets can be like jumping into the great unknown. The public relations professionals at Nelson Communications Group, in Sacramento, take the initiative to learn about their prospects' markets, even if they have no experience with the industry. To convince prospects that the firm is a knowledgeable and trustworthy authority, Nelson Communications holds what it calls "reverse seminars."

"Usually our people go into customer offices to lecture on the details of a news topic that affects the customer," says Donna Lucas, president and CEO. "In a reverse seminar, **we invite corporate experts to lecture us on a news topic**, since that will be an emerging market for us." Recently, a telephone executive briefed Nelson Communications staffers on arcane telecommunications deregulation laws. At another seminar, a public utilities executive and a government regulator discussed the issues involved in important public utilities deregulation. After listening to the experts, staffers are better able to represent companies affected by these issues.

"For us, marketing means really understanding a targeted area we want to be involved in," says Lucas. "And sometimes we've gotten more business from speakers we've invited to lecture, though business development is not the main goal." The seminars are held about twice annually, she adds, and the lecturers, flattered to be asked to present on their area of expertise, usually speak free of charge.

# 184
### IDEA

## How Ya Gonna Keep 'Em Down on the Farm?

**A**fraid that a top-producing sales rep may quit and set up his or her own shop? Many company owners try, first, to draft an airtight noncompete agreement, then get valued reps to sign it. But Gary Bitner, president of Bitner.com, a $2-million marketing and communications company headquartered in Fort Lauderdale, Fla., believes that requiring employees to sign "noncompetes" sets the wrong tone. "They're hard to make work in Florida, anyway," he says. So, as part of his client contract, Bitner **asks customers not to hire or do business with former employees for a year after their departure**.

In California, noncompete agreements are recognized only for shareholders. So Mark Moses, CEO of Platinum Capital Group, a $20-million mortgage banker in Irvine, includes a noncompete clause in the shareholders' agreement his managers sign. If any shareholder leaves while the company is still private, the value of his or her stock will take a 20% "haircut," and Moses can buy back the rest over three years.

# VII

"The phrase *pay for performance* is almost a buzzword these days. But does your company really reward performance? Performance in business doesn't mean trying hard. It means getting the job done."

**PATRICK KELLY**
founder, chairman, and CEO,
PSS/World Medical, Jacksonville, Fla.

# 185
## IDEA

# What's Your Incentive?

**A**s a one-man operation, Michael Bryant, owner of Career Transition Services, in Baltimore, has to keep himself on his toes. He has no employees with families to feed. He has no aggressive managers forcing him to look toward the future. So **to keep himself on track, Bryant instituted sales incentives for himself**.

First, he set up a chart that divided the sources of his revenue into logical categories: individuals, consulting, speeches, and workshops. His goal was to convert more speech customers into consulting customers, since consulting pays more. Then he started playing games, using his data to keep score, just like an open-book company. Bryant set monthly revenue goals and rewarded himself with prizes for making his numbers: a coveted zoom camera in July, a CD-ROM drive for the kids in August ("Dad, are you going to make your number?"), a new freezer in September.

The trick with incentive plans, of course, is to keep them challenging and fresh. So Bryant has begun thinking about nonmonetary forms of compensation, "like giving myself time off for a job well done." In 1998, he is focusing on getting retainers and setting goals for the number of retainers he receives. The upshot is that Bryant has more control over his business. And being in control, as every entrepreneur knows, is fun. "This is how I get pleasure," he says. "When I look at the accounts and say, 'I need to do something to move these numbers,' then I do something and they move. I feel terrific."

# 186
**IDEA**

# Delayed Gratification

**D**esigning an incentive package that is mutually profitable to both the company and its sales representatives can be a real high-wire act. The company wants to hold onto collected funds to ease cash-flow management. Salespeople, understandably, want their commission as soon as they've closed a sale. Cindy Revenaugh hammered out a compromise that has helped propel her Chicago company's sales of pressure-sensitive label paper from $1 million to $14 million since 1987.

Channeled Resources, of which Revenaugh is vice-president, **delays paying a portion of the rep's commission** to accommodate the inevitable ups and downs of sales. "For example," explains Revenaugh, "if salespeople have a base target of $15,000 worth of label paper in a month but only sell $12,000, then the next month they must hit $18,000 in sales. They'll receive 25% of the profits they generate above $18,000." Sales representatives receive commission checks quarterly, but not for the total amount due from the prior quarter. "We give them half of what they earn from the most recent quarter, so if they don't make their numbers the following quarter, we're even. If they hit their numbers the second quarter, they get the second half of what they are owed from the first quarter, plus the first half on the most recent quarter. We catch them up at the end of the year."

The plan also helps keep salespeople loyal. If they quit, they lose whatever commissions are still owed to them in the coming quarter. "Since salespeople are immediate-gratification oriented, they'll work through a slump to receive a commission that's coming to them, rather than sacrifice it and start from scratch at another company," observes Revenaugh.

## Personal Best

**A**nnual sales forecasts can be like the weather: highly unpredictable and due to a variety of unseen factors. Yet NCO Financial Systems, a collections agency in Fort Washington, Pa., habitually meets its aggressive sales goals. The secret: President Chuck Piola **discusses personal goals with each of the sales representatives before setting any company goals or forecasts**.

While one rep may need to earn only $40,000 a year, another may be motivated to earn $75,000. That's fine by Piola, as long as all 25 meet their targets. "It's not important how *much* a representative expects to sell as it is to find out *how*," says Piola. "Are they willing to come in to work on Saturdays? Do they have accounts in the works that could yield those numbers? How many cold calls are they going to make a week?"

These meetings motivate sales representatives as well as stress the importance of meeting their annual goals. Their chances of fulfilling their quotas are much greater if reps set their own targets. "By troubleshooting sales targets at the beginning of the year, we really increase our chances of reaching our corporate revenue goals," says Piola, who has driven NCO's sales from $8 million to $125 million since 1992.

# 188
**IDEA**

## Hitting Pay Dirt

**A**t small, fast-growing businesses, where so much rides on key salespeople, it's important to set up **a compensation strategy that helps achieve long-term goals**. Here's how three *Inc.* 500 companies do it.

&bull; National Patient Care Systems, a medical supplier in South Hackensack, N.J., pays the sales manager 70% of his income needs as base salary, so he won't get complacent. To emphasize growth, CEO Glenn Edwards adds 0.1% of gross revenues up to the previous year's revenues and 0.2% of sales that exceed that figure.

&bull; Shane Jones of Ace Personnel, a $7.3-million staffing service in Overland Park, Kans., admits that his sales manager's base salary is below the industry average, but says, "I ask employees to take some risk." The rewards for risk include annual profit sharing (of which the manager will get about $3,500) and a monthly commission consisting of 2% of gross margins. She's also eligible for a $4,500 quarterly bonus pool that is divvied up among the company's 27 employees.

&bull; Shiraz Balolia of Woodstock International, a $6.5-million manufacturer of woodworking accessories in Bellingham, Wash., paid the sales manager above-average base pay, plus a bonus for making the *Inc.* 500 list of the nation's fastest-growing private companies. After making the list with $4.2 million in 1995 revenues, Balolia paid his sales manager an additional 20% over his base salary.

# 189
**IDEA**

# Role Reversal

Like many professional service companies, Program Management Co. (PMC), in Exton, Pa., relies on the people who know its product best—its technical staff—to push its environmental and information technology services. Unlike many of his rivals, CEO Jack Newell decided that **scientists who act like salespeople should be paid like salespeople** and earn a commission.

Twenty senior scientists and engineers compete for annual bonuses tied to new-business targets, billable hours, and other goals, such as presenting a certain number of technical papers. The bonuses are paid out twice a year, provided the company meets its overall profitability goal.

At PMC, the typical bonus is 25% of a technical staffer's salary, although one exceptional program director raked in 50% after bringing in an extra $3 million in sales and increasing his billable hours. For the fiscal year ending April 1995, the program's best year, PMC paid out $520,000—or almost 29% of pretax net profits. Sales have grown from $3.6 million to $25.9 million.

Is the plan too generous? "Since we meet our goals and have nearly zero percent turnover among scientists, I'm reluctant to change it," says Newell, who supports the incentive program with sales training and a marketing manager.

# Enterprising Wardrobes

**T**he typical college wardrobe doesn't make the grade in a professional work environment. But at St. Louis-based Enterprise Rent-A-Car, where store managers and clerks—primarily recent college grads—don't wear a uniform jacket, a well-groomed appearance is a must. "We want our employees to dress as professionally as a bank teller would, to communicate to customers that branch employees and managers are professionals," says Andy Taylor, the family-owned company's CEO and president.

As a result, many of Enterprise's branches **use clothing certificates as an incentive** for employees who are working their way up the ladder of this sales-driven organization. "Most young people like to shop and look good on the job, and I was no exception. It was a great perk for passing the test," says Christy Conrad, who received a $300 gift certificate to a local department store when she passed a 90-day exam as a management trainee. Since it's each region's decision to use the award, there are no statistics on how much the program has cost Enterprise companywide. However, in terms of morale and image building, local sales managers agree that the program has been worth every penny.

# Turn Motivation Inside Out

**W**orking late, rushing to get a proposal ready for overnight couriers, and shrewd negotiating over the telephone to set up appointments are just a few of the tasks performed by inside sales teams that all too often go unrecognized and unrewarded. This can cause resentment between them and a company's outside reps. Not so at The VINE Co., a fast-growing maker of victim-notification systems in Louisville.

At VINE, the **inside sales-support people are paid commissions** as well. "Our selling cycle can run as long as nine months," says CEO Mike Davis. "The inside sales team works very hard to move the sale along. If we didn't offer these people incentives, our selling cycle could drag out much longer."

Davis reports that the insiders' commission was originally tied to the number of meetings they set up and other intermediate objectives. But that system was scrapped after the meetings they were setting up did not lead to signed contracts. "Since the objective is the same for the inside sales-support staffers as it is for the outside sales reps, we now tie the inside sales commission directly to the performance of the outside sales rep they work with," says Davis. He adds that the outside sales team also makes a conscious effort to call in and give its inside support staffers feedback on how the meetings went, so that they are motivated to keep the ball rolling. The setup is paying off. From a staff of two in 1995, the company has grown so much that it expects to employ 83 people by the end of 1998.

# No-Quota Noncoms

**M**ost companies pay their salespeople some combination of salary and commission. At PROSOFT, a $27-million provider of technical services and training in Virginia Beach, Va., salespeople don't have a quota and don't earn product commissions. Instead, they are on salary and share in year-end profits.

Before the system was instituted, PROSOFT's reps used to focus on what customers (such as government agencies) had budgeted to spend, rather than on those customers' real needs. "I heard from disgruntled customers who needed additional support after going through our training," says cofounder Michael Adolphi. Repeat business dropped; sales fell flat.

Also, PROSOFT's engineers—who helped with sales presentations but got no help preparing lengthy bid proposals—thought commissions were unfair. Adolphi's solution: **Drop all commissions and raise sales salaries** to roughly match the engineers' pay. "The technical people are involved all the time now," says Adolphi. "And the salespeople help with the bids."

PROSOFT made its first-ever profit-sharing contribution to its 401(k) plan and paid all 115 employees a year-end bonus in 1992. A year later, sales compensation had increased 7% on average, sales grew 250%, all contracts were renewed, and PROSOFT secured $20 million in new, multiyear contracts.

# 193
**IDEA**

## Ask What They're Worth

When John Sample, CEO of Business Interiors, shifted his company from a "lone ranger" approach to a "team-based" organization, one of the scariest aspects was figuring out the compensation system for the sales force. He spent a lot of time pondering what was fair.

To get some answers that everyone could accept, the company conducted **a wage-and-salary survey**, which has become an annual event for the office-furniture dealership in Irving, Tex. Sample asked sales teams to submit proposals on the type and level of compensation they'd like to be paid. "We weren't far apart when we finally did that. It was really one of the smallest problems when I got down to it," he says. Sample worked out a system that includes individual incentives for salespeople out calling on customers and rewards for the entire sales team when certain profitability levels are reached.

# 194

**IDEA**

## More Bucks for the Bang

**Y**our product line is broad, but your reps want to sell their old favorites. What do you do? Listen to the CEO of a company famous for its acoustic guitars. To grow profitably, Washburn International, in Vernon Hills, Ill., must also sell its other products, such as professional audio equipment. To keep his 18 domestic salespeople tuned in to the full line, CEO Rudy Schlacher offers this incentive: Meet the goal for all product categories and **earn an extra 1% commission "override" on all products sold** during that month.

After three months, 20% of the reps earned the override; a year later, 75% did—with Schlacher's guidance. "If they've satisfied one goal, I encourage them to go on to categories where they've met only 40% of their goal and where I have more stock," he explains.

In the program's first year, Schlacher attributes 10% of the company's 31% growth to the incentive program. Inventory turnover went up 20%, saving $70,000 a year in interest costs. Instead of sitting on inventory and back orders, Schlacher says, "I'm able to deliver more product to my customer," resulting in 1997 sales of $58 million.

"Bringing out the best in people means appreciating what they do, rewarding them for it, and giving them the role models they need to become top performers."

**ZIG ZIGLAR**
CEO, Zig Ziglar Corp., Carrollton, Tex., and author of
*Top Performance* (Berkley Books)

# 195
**IDEA**

## Instant Rewards for Long-Term Releases

**C**onverting a customer from purchase orders to a long-term contract takes a lot of your sales force's time, and it's more stressful to sell to the client's management than to employees who authorize single orders. Plus, the excitement of landing a new contract often fades when salespeople have to wait months for commissions to kick in. "I could never figure out why my salespeople never smiled when they got their commission checks," confesses Steve Braccini, former president and CEO of Pro Fasteners, an Austin, Tex., seller of industrial hardware and inventory control services.

Instead of making salespeople wait until revenues rolled in, Braccini paid a **fat commission check up front when a customer switched to a contract**. Within a week or so, the salesperson received a check amounting to six months' commissions on the contract. To estimate the contract's worth, Braccini and the sales rep would consider the customer's previous six months of purchases and projections for the next six. If a one-year contract was valued at $50,000, the rep got $1,250, or half of the 5% commissions he or she would collect later.

The check was like a signing bonus, "a reward for converting the account," says Braccini. "There was instant gratification." On top of base pay and commissions on purchase orders, salespeople netted, on average, an extra $2,500 per month in bonuses. The pay-policy change boosted Pro Fasteners' efforts to convert customers to contracts. When Braccini sold the company at the end of 1996, about 65% of his business was done that way.

# 196
## IDEA

# Honor Thy Colleague

The sales meeting crackled with bonus money. ABL Electronics, a $12-million cable assemblies company in Hunt Valley, Md., had reported a great month, and its 16 sales reps were a little richer. They shared the wealth with the company's buyer and production manager, who were recipients of the team's highest honor: "Phantom Sales Rep of the Month."

**All 72 employees are eligible for this most-valuable-player award**, given to about five employees of the sales team's choosing each month. The higher the company's gross profit goes beyond breakeven, the more money is evenly split among the salaried sales reps and the "phantoms." Depending on the month's sales, the bonus ranges from $250 to $3,000 per person.

"It's pretty exciting when a production manager at a sales-driven company can win," notes sales vice-president Bill Litsinger. That month, the two employees honored had made it possible to ship one big order after another. At other times, the sales force has also singled out the receptionist (for record number of proposals sent out) and workers in order entry, manufacturing, and customer service.

# Carrots on a Stick

**S**ome salespeople have been with you for years, others only months. How do you motivate both camps? Peripheral Enhancements, in Ada, Okla., has **incentives for the year, quarter, month, week, and even for the hour**. "I have a bonus plan in place at all times," says Jeff Thompson, president of the $72-million manufacturer of computer-memory products. While some of Thompson's best performers among his 24 salespeople thrive by working toward quarterly and yearly goals, others, particularly the newcomers, respond better to daily stimuli.

His most effective sales contests reinforce the value of staying in touch with customers. For example, when Thompson buys a large quantity of computer-memory parts at a great price, he runs an "overstock" contest— for so many lots sold over a certain price, the salesperson puts his or her name in a hat to win $100. It's an incentive to get salespeople to call old clients, as well as cold-call prospects, about the latest bargain.

Many of the bonuses are tied to gross profit rather than sales volume. On certain days, the person who contributes the most to the gross profit wins an extra $100 to $500. To make it easier for salespeople to offer attractive prices without cutting too far into profits, Thompson posts a chart that lists the cost to his company of popular items; the staff can check the computer for product costs, too.

# 198
## IDEA

# High Stakes, No Steaks

Call Andy Duke cheap. If his salespeople wine and dine potential customers, the salespeople pick up the tab. And they pay for their gas and car phones. Duke is co-owner of Metrographics, a $5.2-million printing services company in Fairfield, N.J. He developed his penny-pinching ways when he quit NCR and started Metrographics with just $300. That was in 1987, but the **no-expenses-paid policy** endures.

Still, Duke's seven salespeople aren't grumbling. They keep 50% of the gross profit on every sale, and there's no ceiling on commissions. They, not Duke, select their territories and accounts. "We wanted them to immediately think smart, as if they owned the business," says Duke. Once a salesperson surpasses $100,000 in commissions, his or her payout jumps to 60% of the margin on each sale.

"The salesperson wins, and the company wins," says Denise Koper, who left a good customer-service job in Boston to join Metrographics' sales team. "When we find the right people, there's no reason for them to go anywhere else," claims Duke. The system has its limitations, however. "I can't attract a heavy-hitter salesperson who needs the security of $50,000 up front," says Duke.

# Equity Beats Commission

John Strelitz, president of paper broker Streco Fibres, in Virginia Beach, Va., looks for deals such as buying scrap magazine stock and selling it to the gift-wrap market. Strelitz's best deal, though, is one he made for two promising salespeople.

Looking to diversify, Strelitz spun off a second company, Pyramid Paper Products, which warehoused and processed paper in Hot Springs, Ark. He gave Robert Hortman and John McMinamin, two young guns with vital industry contacts, each a 20% **ownership stake in lieu of commissions or big salaries**. The two, then 33 and 38, drove Pyramid's sales, but also got more responsibility for running the business.

"Being part owners made them smarter about purchasing, collection, the quality of accounts, and cash flow," says Strelitz. "They acted like partners."

Five years later, when Pyramid was up and running, Streco reabsorbed it. "Start out by planning when to take over the spinoff company *before* it begins to compete with its parent," cautions Strelitz. In 1997, Streco hit $13 million in sales.

**200 IDEA**

# All on the Same Team

**T**oo often, the sales department can seem isolated from the rest of the company. In part to integrate sales with the rest of the business, Chris MacAllister, president of MacAllister Machinery, a distributor of Caterpillar tractors in Indianapolis, designed a **bonus plan that encourages his five managers—including the sales director—to collaborate**. "I wanted the managers to work more as a team—at problem solving, generating incremental revenue, and customer service," he says.

The bonus goals MacAllister devised with his managers were based on one-third of pretax profit dollars, one-third pretax profit margin, and one-third total sales. Profit dollars were related to what the company could put into retained earnings and profit sharing, profit margin was related to the managers' efficiency in running their departments, and sales volume was related to market share.

The plan was an all-or-nothing proposition for the managers: They all won, or they all lost. The bonus amount differed from manager to manager as a percentage of salary, and there were no caps.

"Before, the sales department interacted with parts and service only when necessary," MacAllister says. "This program brought the sales manager closer. He set the tone for the sales force; it cascaded down."

MacAllister knew the program was working when two repeat customers gave him 100% of their business for machines, parts, and service after his managers teamed up on sales calls. "That wouldn't have happened if we called on them separately," he says. Not only did the managers meet their goals, they "blew them away," earning bonuses approaching 50% of salary and helping the company emerge from an industrywide slump.

## Activity Is a Bonus

If you know what steps it takes to make a sale in your industry, why not reward salespeople for following those steps? At ESP Systems Professionals, a $5-million executive search firm in Minneapolis, about **20% of the base compensation of a new sales hire is activity based**. ESP tracks three activities weekly: daily calls to potential job candidates, company visits, and "balls in the air"—leads that could convert to sales. President Bob Hildreth used ESP's best salespeople as a benchmark for his activity list.

A salesperson who meets the goals can earn, on top of salary, up to $400 a month in bonuses. Placing an average of 30 calls a day reaps a $100 bonus for that month; making three company visits a week also nets $100. One to four balls in the air weekly is good for an additional $100. Doing all of the above brings in another $100.

Hildreth admits the bonus program is a risk, but a calculated one. The six reps who followed the regimen are still with ESP, billing on average about 200% more than the industry norm. Part of the reason? The program focuses the sales training process and gives new salespeople more confidence. Making 30 to 40 calls daily "really helped establish a network, which gave me lots of referrals," says one salesperson.

**202**

**IDEA**

# Where Do You Stand?

**W**hen should you hire a salesperson? When should you hire more salespeople? How do you establish a sales compensation plan—or fine-tune the one you have to make your salespeople more productive? How do you write meaningful job descriptions? Set quotas?

These are among the **many sales-management issues addressed** in *What America's Small Companies Pay Their Sales Forces...And How They Make It Pay Off*, by Christen P. Heide (Dartnell, 800-621-5463, 1997, $39.95). Based on a survey of nearly 300 companies with sales of less than $5 million—and employing a total of more than 2,000 salespeople—the book is divided into two parts: Part 1 covers sales compensation basics, incentive programs, territory design, quota-setting, and job descriptions; Part 2 presents benchmark data against which you can measure your company's sales management policies—levels of pay, expenses, benefits, training, how salespeople spend their time, and a profile of "today's sales force."

There's an introductory section on frequently asked questions about sales management, which ends with the question, "What if I have a question that isn't answered in this book?" The answer: You can contact the author at the 800 number above, ext. 3142. Heide will try to find an answer—and probably use it in his next book.

# One for All, All for Profit

**D**ave Jones knew his people were "smart enough to get clients, keep them happy, and make a profit." He had a problem, however. "A $100,000 project could cost $200,000 to execute," says Jones, president of Human Resources Consulting Group, a division of Aon Consulting, in Detroit. The reason, Jones realized, was that he wasn't paying employees to make a profit.

In 10 years of fast growth, the firm's pretax profit margins rarely dipped below 10%, but there wasn't enough money left for research and development. So Jones decided to **stop paying new-account bonuses**. Instead, he inaugurated a profit-sharing plan for everyone—including new salespeople.

Each of the company's offices is a profit center, rewarded on its own income statement; office directors can use up to 30% of the profits to reward "special players." Otherwise, bonuses are based on a percentage of salary.

Within two years of starting the new system, Jones was able to distribute $500,000 among his 150 employees. A few of the company's senior consultants—industrial psychologists who doubled as salespeople—favored the old volume-based sales bonuses and left. But most, Jones says, were relieved to share responsibility for sales.

# Clearance Sale

**W**hen Channeled Resources, a Chicago company that sells recycled paper products, gets stuck with slow-moving inventory, sales vice-president Cindy Revenaugh turns the problem into a solution. She tells her sales force they can **sell inventory at any price they want as long as it's not below cost**. As an incentive, the salespeople get 10% of the sale.

The company has a policy of taking inventory over a two-month period for this program. "Normally," says Revenaugh, "they wouldn't earn an incentive on a per-sale basis, because they work on team incentives. We just want to move the stuff and get cash for it. Even if they sell it at cost, it's better than letting it sit here. Our salespeople have the flexibility to figure out what they can get for it. We've probably moved $100,000 worth of inventory that way, exceeding expectations by 25%." With 1997 revenues of $13 million, Revenaugh is happy about it, and so are the salespeople, who are earning more than what they would usually get paid.

"Our goals are always based
on the security of the company
and its future. If we fail to reach
a goal, the company is at risk.
Each goal is a must, not a want."

**JACK STACK**
president and CEO,
Springfield ReManufacturing Corp.,
Springfield, Mo.

## Combat Medals

**S**alespeople who excel deserve to be recognized. In fact, salespeople who triumph in the face of personal danger, who risk their well-being for the sake of the company, deserve a prize.

Brent Bingham, CEO of Eclipse Marketing, in Provo, Utah, created an award in honor of salesman Nathan Berrett, who was attacked by a German shepherd dog while peddling pest-control products door to door. The **prize "for giving your all and then some"** is bestowed each year.

Winners are chosen by applause at the year-end meeting, at which candidates recount harrowing sales experiences. "It creates lore and legend within the company," says Bingham. Berrett, now recovered, has the honor of presenting the award. To find road-warrior candidates for a similar award in your company, you have only to ask them to share their horror stories.

# Ring Up the Spirit

**W**hen PCs Compleat, a reseller of brand-name PCs through catalogs and direct-response advertising, opened its doors, the founders installed a huge boxing-ring bell they had bought at an auction. The bell was rung whenever a sale was made. "When the bell rang, you'd see all these people scurrying out, asking, 'Whadda ya got?'" said Kevin Abbott, an early employee at the Marlborough, Mass., company. Hearing the bell, Abbott said, provided "reassurance that things were happening."

But when PCs Compleat's revenues began climbing, all the clanging got to be a headache. So the bell was saved for team-building occasions, such as **contests designed to pull people from other departments onto the sales floor**.

Once or twice a month, a salesperson who had just gotten an order rang the bell and picked the name of another employee out of a hat. The lucky person was summoned down to Sales, where a basketball hoop awaited. The salesperson and the coworker decided who would shoot the basket. A swoosh (in three tries) netted each person $10. Whatever the game, the contest recalled the early days.

PCs Compleat backed up its all-for-one message by letting all employees log on to the sales-tracking system to see how the sales force was doing daily, weekly, or quarterly. "We believed that if people have an awareness of sales and their part in them, the company would work better," says former president and COO Jack Littman-Quinn. It worked: The company's sales stood at more than $250 million when it was sold to CompUSA, in May 1996.

# 207
## IDEA

# And the Winner Is...

USF Seko Worldwide, a freight-forwarding company in Elk Grove, Ill., has a novel way of deciding who gets new computers on a limited technology budget: The $106-million company runs an **essay contest to award equipment upgrades**. Eighty of its independent sales reps competed for 20 fully loaded Toshiba Satellite Pro laptops by explaining why the writer should get one and how it would benefit both the rep and the company.

"We wanted to make sure we were giving the computers to the right people," explains Cathy Moran, Seko's director of sales training and support. "We got a lot of very creative responses." One rep gave the laptop a name and told a story from its perspective. Another recorded a song, to the tune of the "Beverly Hillbillies" theme: "This is a story about a man named Bob, whose computer was so slow, he could hardly do his job." Top-40 material it wasn't, but the guy got his laptop—with the expectation that it would help him make more sales.

## 208
### IDEA

# A Taste of Creativity

**W**hen it comes to brainstorming sessions, burnt coffee and an old conference table can really dampen enthusiasm. Memories of previous meetings in the room may discourage employees from putting forth creative proposals. To liven things up, DEI, a Cincinnati-area architectural and construction company, runs **special events to generate sales ideas**.

For one session, which was not mandatory, vice-president Cynthia Grow held a wine tasting. She says that the event drew employees to the meeting and helped them relax before getting down to the business of figuring out how to increase sales at the $31.8-million company. Grow also asks employees to prepare in creative ways: Before the wine tasting, they had to read a trade magazine from another industry and extrapolate ideas for a current DEI project.

**209**
**IDEA**

# A Doughnut for Your Thoughts

To keep staffers up-to-date and pave the way for a new product or promotion, herd them into the conference room: Making a speech once is more efficient than repeating it 30 times, and calling a formal meeting drives home the importance of an issue better than a memo. The problem lies in getting people there—especially at retail businesses where many employees work different shifts. That's why Penny and Frank Burkard, co-owners of Burkard Nurseries, in Pasadena, Calif., hold quarterly **breakfast meetings for their staff** of 30 part-timers.

"Working part-time, employees can feel disconnected from the organization," says Penny Burkard. "These meetings help bring everyone together so that we are all working with the same information. Recently, we held one before the busy rose-selling season to bring employees up to speed on the new stock and how to sell it."

To make sure employees take the meetings seriously, the Burkards hire a facilitator to work through the agenda. And why breakfast? They can't afford to close down the store during working hours, and evening meetings were not practical: Employees might be burned out, get stuck in traffic, or have another obligation and not show up. "It's not easy getting here for a 6:30 a.m. meeting," says Burkard, "but the wake-up call makes them more committed to the company and revs them up for the sales mission."

**210**
IDEA

# Prize Fighter

**U**nshakable confidence is a good quality in a salesperson who wrangles with competitors, but it may become problematic in dealing with customers and colleagues. In fact, such people often have exceedingly fragile egos. Michael Rosenberg, president of Horizon Foods, a $30-million national home-foods service company in Plainview, N.Y., finds that opening up lines of communication is crucial in managing temperamental salespeople.

Rosenberg's first step in getting through to combative employees is **demonstrating that the boss is really on the employee's side**. The process is sometimes best initiated outside the office. "I take them fishing. I have them over to my house, and I have my house set up for that purpose. I have my kids play with their kids and my wife spend time with their wives." Once a rapport is established, Rosenberg says, he tries to address abrasive behavior as a problem to be solved jointly, rather than a personality flaw the employee must fix on his or her own. To that end, when problems come up, he literally swaps chairs with the employee and asks him or her to pretend to be the boss for a minute: "If you were in my shoes, how would you handle this?"

**IDEA**

# Cheer Leader

**H**ave you neglected to keep your sales staff motivated while you're managing crises and pushing goals? **Put encouragement on your "must-do" list.** Just write the names of people who report to you on your weekly agenda. Then cross them off when you catch them "doing something right" relative to their performance goals, and acknowledge it.

To remind himself to thank people as part of his daily routine, Hyler Bracey, a consultant with Right Management Consultants, in Philadelphia, places five coins in his pocket every morning. During the day, he'll transfer a coin to another pocket every time he praises an employee for good work. This approach works particularly well for no-nonsense executive types who like to focus on getting things done.

**212**

**IDEA**

# Complimentary Tickets

**A**ppreciation from managers is one of the incentives that salespeople value most. And yes, even busy entrepreneurs can find ways to **make praising employees a habit**. Here are three simple techniques:

❧ *Write notes at the end of the day.* Steve Wittert, CEO of $4-million Ziro Design, in San Diego, is seldom able to take time out to compliment his staff, who designs and manufactures contemporary clocks. Instead, he keeps a stack of notecards and takes a few minutes to jot personal notes to deserving individuals before he leaves the office.

❧ *Let technology carry the message.* Use voice mail to praise your sales staff. One company created an "Applause" bulletin board on its e-mail system, so that anyone can post a thank-you to a coworker.

❧ *Practice group recognition.* Bob Nelson, president of Nelson Motivation, in San Diego, recommends starting a staff meeting by reading a letter of thanks or praise from a customer. You can also create a "wall of fame" to show appreciation for top achievers—or keep "successful projects" scrapbooks to record team accomplishments. Exhibit the book prominently in your lobby.

# 213
**IDEA**

## Clip Joint

**A**s a junior high school history teacher, Chuck Piola became an expert at motivating people to learn and grow. Now he uses those same techniques to help grow his collections agency, NCO Financial Systems, in Fort Washington, Pa. One of his favorite "classroom" tactics is to **clip and circulate articles from sales and marketing magazines and newsletters** to the company's 25 sales reps at least once a month. "I like them to see what other people are saying about the same topic I've been talking about," explains Piola.

Piola observes that most people tend to forget the basics at times, or they stop trying to become better at what they do. The articles motivate his sales reps to excel at their work. "Recently, I sent out an article about selling with passion. I put a note on the top, circled three things, and circulated it to my sales guys with a note, 'thinking of you.' One of my reps wrote back, 'I read the article, and you are right on the money.' They get energized by the example, and it gives them something positive to talk about at the water cooler."

# 214
**IDEA**

## Flowery Wallpaper

Tom Siebel, chairman and CEO of Siebel Systems, in San Mateo, Calif., wanted to make sure that employees were keeping customers in mind. So he **plastered the office walls with customer paraphernalia**. He decorated the lobby with client logos, and the halls are covered with framed letters and annual reports from clients.

Siebel even named conference and training rooms after his clients. In addition to reminding employees that customers are number one, the decor yields another important payoff: "Customers walk in and see their logo in the lobby and their name on the conference door," says Siebel, whose $120-million company sells sales-force automation software. "They know that we value their business."

**215**

**IDEA**

# Strategic Space

These days, more and more customers don't just want reliable service—they expect solutions to their problems. In advertising, for example, in addition to a clever ad and a smart media buy, clients want their ad agency to increase market share for them.

GSD&M, in Austin, Tex., counts blue-chippers such as Wal-Mart and Southwest Airlines among its 22 customers and boasts a 90% retention rate. Part of GSD&M's pitch to prospects: measurable goals. To assure prospects that their goals will be paramount for the agency, it sets up a **war room plastered with each client's paraphernalia, which functions as command central for the team** working on the account.

War rooms are painted in the client's colors; red phones, used exclusively for conversations with the client, dot the tables. Up on the wall are the client's earnings reports, stock price, newspaper clippings, competitive analyses, and weekly sales figures. War rooms give employees a mental edge and remind them to keep their eyes on the prize, that is, the client's success. Just in case anyone doesn't get it, GSD&M hands out bonuses when customers achieve *their* goals, not when the agency achieves its own. And it's no surprise that clients, too, like the war rooms. The number was increased from three to eight when the agency moved into new quarters, and its billings have grown sixfold since 1988.

**216**

IDEA

# Wall Eyed

**O**nce health-care reform was in the air, cost containment became the watchword of providers. PSS/World Medical, a Jacksonville-based distributor of supplies for nursing homes, imaging centers, and doctors' offices, had to become a low-cost supplier while maintaining the top-level service that had made its reputation. Companies rarely make that kind of change easily, but at PSS, the employees made it work. What motivated their cooperation?

PSS has long had **a share-the-wealth, share-the-information culture**. Every salesperson is a shareholder; some have more than a million dollars' worth of stock in their ESOPs. Branch offices paper a considerable portion of their walls with financial information: what each salesperson sold yesterday, how much gross margin each of them realized, and how the branch is doing, week by week and month by month. The P&L wallpaper, visible to customers, creates an environment that makes it impossible for employees to be cynical about the management's motives or actions.

Critical to the success of the strategic shift, contends CEO Patrick Kelly, was that he didn't just open the books when the crisis came; he'd had them open all along, so that when it came time to buckle down, employees were willing to do their share. When the government was considering health-care reform, PSS's customers, uncertain about its effect on them, became very aware of costs. "And we had to become more conscious of costs," explains Kelly. "Our employees were willing and able to make that change because they had all the information they needed."

**217**

**IDEA**

# Graphic Demonstration

John Westrum's home-building company in Fort Washington, Pa., was growing like mad: From 1991 to 1994, its revenues skyrocketed 700% to $28 million. Paradoxically, the demands of such rapid growth made it impossible for Westrum Development Co. to perform at the level of its own high standards. "Customers were unhappy, contractors were screaming at us, and our management of invoices and payments broke down," recalls Westrum.

Putting their heads together on a retreat, Westrum and his 30 employees developed an 11-point plan that measured the duration of construction projects, the quality of the job according to a 178-point checklist, customers' willingness to recommend Westrum to their friends, and other guidelines. As an incentive to employees, Westrum set up a bonus pool that would be paid out quarterly for meeting intermediate and ultimate customer-retention goals.

The first year, only 20% of the pool was paid out. Then Westrum **posted spreadsheets showing performance over the previous four quarters**. "Employees started focusing not so much on the dollars but on the results," he reports. "Anytime we weren't meeting an objective, people would rally behind the person who needed help. After about a year and a half, the effect was phenomenal." By 1996, 80% of the available pool had already been paid out at the end of the first quarter. Best of all, 90% of customers said they would recommend Westrum to a friend, as opposed to 50% two years earlier.

# 218
### IDEA

## Forecast: Sunny, Breezy, and Clear

**A**t Springfield Remanufacturing, a company in Springfield, Mo., that overhauls truck parts, production problems do not sabotage the sales forecast. CEO Jack Stack makes sure to prevent disappointment by having sales representatives deliver the sales forecast to the company's various divisions.

"The key ingredient of any forecast is passion, which comes from a sense of ownership, a feeling of personal responsibility for the results," says Stack. "**Use your salespeople to link your workforce to the marketplace.** Make sure they understand that jobs depend on their forecast. I want salespeople to be thinking about what impact their numbers will have on the lives of their fellow employees. I also want our inside employees to appreciate the competitive issues we're dealing with. Who better to teach them than our salespeople?"

Each fall, the sales department meets for two days to hash out the numbers. Salespeople chip in what they've learned—everything from new products that engineers should be working on to what the competition is paying for labor. After the marathon meeting, the salespeople report back to their respective divisions. Since 1993, the system has enabled Springfield Remanufacturing to meet its goal of 15% growth annually. In 1997, sales approached $120 million.

**219**
IDEA

# Filling the Blanks

There's nothing like vague communication to gum up a company's operations and ruin customer relationships. Just ask the folks at EconoPrint, in Madison, Wis. In 1993, when the company went from eight printing facilities to a centralized production operation with eight quick-print shops, the customer-service person couldn't walk to the back room anymore and explain something to the press person. "It became a nightmare," says co-owner Dave Roloff. Customers were taking their business elsewhere as orders were either left unfilled until morning or done incorrectly.

Roloff and CEO Patrick Leamy decided to have those responsible for the communication breakdown solve the problem. When **employees design their own customer-order form**, they are more likely to fill it out accurately, avoiding gaps in customer service.

First, the company had its 60 employees fill out a survey, responding to the question, "What are the five biggest obstacles to doing your job correctly?" Then individual departments met with Leamy and Roloff to discuss how to improve customer service. Each department elected one person to represent it at the next meeting. The representatives were asked what they needed to know to answer every question their department might have about an order. With that information, they were able to design a one-page order form.

EconoPrint's customer-order form has been so effective in detailing the work process that out of roughly 5,000 jobs completed monthly, fewer than 10 come under question. Tighter controls have meant greater net profits: They rose 34% in 1993 and have risen nearly 10% every year since.

# Uniform Sales Support

To help grow sales of a tired industrial laundry company he acquired, Joe Giezeman knew he needed every single employee on his side. At his Searcy Industrial Laundry, **everyone who isn't on the road selling new accounts wears a uniform** to help build morale and promote team spirit. That includes the owner, who sports a popular executive outfit: navy-blue slacks and a sky-blue short-sleeved shirt, with the company name on one side and "Joe" on the other. Giezeman likes being in uniform because it's easy, neat, and it helps make the point that at his company, the owner and the employees are a team. And uniforms convey a positive impression to the public.

Under Giezeman and his wife Kathy, the laundry, located in Searcy, Ark., has prospered. Annual sales have risen to more than $6 million, with pretax profits approaching 10%.

**221**

**IDEA**

# Hedge Your Bet

**W**hat is a company without sales? Out of business. That's why many business owners are afraid to turn over valued client relationships to a newly recruited representative or manager. To reduce the risk of losing customers during the transition, Kevin Owens, a sportswear producer in Burlington, Vt., hit upon a way to hedge his bet: **Hand over some—but not all—of the key accounts to the new sales manager**. The arrangement put some healthy pressure on the manager to prove he could bring in new customers (he did), and it allowed Owens to keep a hand in the growth of Select Design, which projects sales of $4 million in 1998.

Another way to minimize the risk is—don't shudder—to make the sales manager a shareholder. That way, the new hire is tied more tightly to your company than to your prized customers. And if you have the sales manager/shareholder sign a noncompete agreement, it stands a much better chance of holding up in court.

**222**

**IDEA**

# School of Hard Knocks

**T**o teach one of his managers the difference between good and bad sales, Norm Brodsky took him cold-calling for a day. The manager insisted he couldn't sell. Brodsky showed him that anyone could sell. All you have to do is cut your price. "But that's not a *good* sale," he said. "My definition of a good sale involves making money on it. When we hire salespeople, we're paying them to go out and make sales *at a profit*."

Brodsky, who owns CitiStorage, a business-document archival and retrieval service in Brooklyn, N.Y., insists that **it's important for key managers to make sales calls a couple of days a month**. "A kind of mystique develops in a company," he says. "When salespeople say that they can't sell your product at full price, that the market is demanding a steep discount or a special deal, managers don't know how to respond. They don't trust themselves. The salesperson could be right or wrong, but the people who have to decide don't have a clue."

By having managers make those decisions, a company maintains control over the profitability of a sale, but the managers can only make good decisions if they've been out in the market. There, they get to know who their customers are, why their company is different from the competition, and what changes it could make that would allow it to earn a premium. "Managers need to understand all that if they're going to play a significant role in setting company policy, but they won't learn it unless someone takes the trouble to teach them," adds Brodsky. That, of course, is where the company owner comes in.

# Be There, or Be Square

**A**s vice-president of Channeled Resources, a Chicago company that sells pressure-sensitive label paper, Cindy Revenaugh does everything in her power to get her sales reps to hang up the phone and hit the road. She encourages them to **call on accounts in person** by providing an ample car allowance and placing no limit on travel and entertainment expenses.

"None of our seven salespeople travel the way I'd like them to. They like working the phone better," says Revenaugh. "Some people are really comfortable going home every night. If you don't go face-to-face, you don't find out about new projects lying on a customer's desk or discover what the competition is doing. You don't get the whole story over the phone."

Recently, Revenaugh discovered that a customer was looking for a specialty security tape that her company didn't carry. She made a couple of phone calls and found two new sources for it. She was also able to hook the customer up with another customer that she had seen earlier in the week.

"There's no way I would have been able to put together those sales if I wasn't there in person. It's that kind of brainstorming that builds a solid customer relationship," says Revenaugh, who clocks more than 30,000 miles a year on the road. "I'm always on the road, and our revenues are always growing"—from less than $1 million to more than $14 million annually.

# 224
## IDEA

# Keep On Truckin'

**W**hen Patrick Kelly founded PSS/World Medical, in 1983, most doctors bought supplies from companies selling to hospitals and nursing homes, but the suppliers' big trucks would only make a delivery once a week. The next-day service offered by PSS was a novelty and a competitive differentiator. Then Kelly decided to go after his biggest competitor, Taylor Medical. He put a salesperson into Beaumont, Tex., the competitor's home base, even though he knew that the rep wouldn't make any sales at first. PSS also sent in a truck every day, regardless of whether it had an order in Beaumont. "But there's nothing to deliver," exclaimed the local manager. "The driver thinks you're crazy!"

Kelly explained his reasoning: "We wanted the salesman to see that van going to Beaumont every day. He'd know it was his responsibility to fill it up. Also, that truck had to go every day, regardless of whether it was empty, because we never wanted to offer anything less than same-day service." The sight of **an empty van in his territory every day motivated the salesperson to crack the competitor's market**.

PSS, which is based in Jacksonville, Fla., now has a branch in Beaumont that does $5 million a year—and back in 1995, it acquired competitor Taylor Medical.

# 225
## IDEA

# Numbers Pool

**P**eople who work at home or alone in a branch office often find it hard to maintain discipline during the day. Brian Rice of Marblehead, Mass., **keeps the pressure on himself by teaming up with another sales rep** to meet collaborative quotas.

Rice and his partner in Sun Dog Sales, which represents five sportswear and sunglasses manufacturers nationwide, work in separate offices, each selling to 200 outlets throughout New England. To push and pace themselves, they split the work and pool their earnings. Every month, they e-mail the previous month's numbers to each other. Rice, for example, tries to write $3,000 in sales contracts each day. If the afternoon is waning and he's falling short, he'll keep working.

The daily pressure the partners put on themselves, and the monthly pressure they put on each other, has helped Sun Dog grow to $3 million in sales in eight years. The duo also increases its quotas annually. "We have two different personalities and two different ways of selling," says Rice. "The quotas are the best way for us to reach mutual goals."

# 226
**IDEA**

## Pick-up Service Picks Up Sales

**A**s companies grow, their need to maintain brand identity and long-term goals can crush employee initiative. One way to build a cohesive organization with decentralized locations is to **include middle managers in the traditional, annual top-management retreat**. That's what St. Louis-based Enterprise Rent-A-Car does. Every year, all branch managers—from 3,500 branches in 1998—assemble to discuss corporate goals, swap problem-solving strategies, and discover emerging market trends. During the day, breakout sessions explore various aspects of managing an agency. In the evening, social events encourage additional conversation.

One outcome of the expanded retreats has become legendary. A branch manager reported that for many customers, getting a ride to and from the car-rental agency was a big hassle. He began offering complimentary pick-up and drop-off service—at nominal cost, since most customers lived within 15 minutes of his agency. The service was a boon to his sales. At a subsequent annual management meeting, it was reported that 30% of the branches had adopted the shuttle service with equal success. The company then made it standard operating procedure and used it for its slogan, "Pick Enterprise. We'll pick you up."

# 227
**IDEA**

# New-Product Survival Strategies

**W**hen Milwaukee-based Koss Corp., a $40-million stereo-head-phone maker, decided to enter the promising new market of computer headphones and speakers, sales vice-president John Koss Jr. realized that nurturing an unpredictable **new product line requires more disciplined sales management**.

&. *Recruiting sales staff*. Koss's longtime reps excelled at selling to stereo shops, but few had experience with computer stores. Rather than retraining them, Koss hired six computer-rep firms to sell PC headphones and speakers in several key markets. "There was this whole other world of reps I didn't know about," he says. "You love the ones who have buyers' home phone numbers."

&. *Forecasting sales*. "When you're in a hot market, you have to look at the big picture," says Koss. He kept close tabs on the size of the multimedia market, both home and corporate. He also focused on the smaller "micro" trends that affect key accounts. Sales and inventory data from retail and OEM (original equipment manufacturer) accounts enabled him to analyze the sales of mass-merchants versus superstores. The data also enabled him to isolate inventory turnover by item, month, and retail outlet. Koss prepared three sales forecasts: "regular," "stretch," and "bomb."

&. *Managing inventory*. Koss worked closely with manufacturing, adjusting forecasts on a monthly basis. He learned to stick to the plan, to the point of even turning down some "big deals" because there wasn't the inventory.

Koss's disciplined sales management paid off: Within three years, sales of computer accessories grew to 25% of total revenues.

# Sizing Up Sales Hang-Ups

**W**ant to find out why your people don't sell more? David Kurlan, a seasoned sales management expert and a principal at Objective Management Group, in Southborough, Mass., eschews psychological tests. "They give you the makeup of a person, but they don't tell you whether that person will sell," he says. And skill-based training often doesn't remedy the problems that separate the perennial contenders from the stars. So Kurlan has identified **some classic weaknesses in salespeople**.

1. *Queasiness discussing money.* Some salespeople crumble under the weight of a big deal. Kurlan knew a $50,000-a-year salesperson who was actually worth $200,000 a year once he got past his money block.

2. *Need for approval.* "Some people go into sales to make friends," says Kurlan. "They live for the words 'We really like you.'" But reps who live for approval don't take necessary risks to win a sale. Most salespeople crave acceptance, so this is a most difficult hurdle to leap.

3. *Weak self-assurance.* Salespeople who tell themselves, "It's okay not to close," won't excel until they change the message. The primary goal of a sales visit is to close the deal.

4. *Emotional involvement.* Salespeople who lose their cool are not hearing the customer. How to overcome touchiness? Even good listeners need occasional lessons in levelheadedness.

Here's one way to test sales candidates: Treat each applicant like a cold caller. "In 20 minutes of pressure, you'll see how emotionally involved the person gets," says Kurlan.

# 229
**IDEA**

## Running on Time

**A**s companies expand, managers often find it more difficult to **keep track of how well salespeople are using their time on the road** to visit prospects and customers. Many managers find that phone contact with their salespeople isn't sufficient.

If you're anxious for timely feedback, take a tip from Marilyn Ounjian, CEO of Careers USA, a $30-million staffing company in Boca Raton, Fla. She keeps tabs on reps by having them supplement phoned-in updates with hard copy that managers can critique. Her 70 sales reps update a one-page report listing the basics of each site visit—the client's name and phone number, the rep's time in and out, and what was accomplished. It works, notes Ounjian, because it's filled out and faxed back to branches within 30 seconds.

**230**

**IDEA**

# Same Day, Same Day Planner

**M**etaphorically and in practice, everyone's on the same page at The Phelps Group, a Santa Monica, Calif., integrated marketing-communications company where almost all 56 employees carry the same model of day planner book. How does a **uniform time-management system** inspire salespeople? For starters, the organized format can help prevent them from getting bogged down in paperwork, so it's easier for them to make outgoing calls. Second, having the same day planners connects them to the rest of the organization so that salespeople function as team players.

The system Phelps swears by is called Priority Manager, from Priority Management Systems. "At $495 per employee, it's a big investment—but I think the payoff happens pretty quickly," says CEO Joe Phelps. The cost includes several training sessions, including one in which a trainer walks through a workday with the employee to help establish better time-budgeting behavior. The system melds a calendar of events (meetings, appointments, project deadlines), a daily scheduler, an A-to-Z directory with phone numbers, a communications planner, and a special scheduler for "balance elements" (soccer games, pottery class, symphony concerts). "It's become a part of the company culture," says Phelps. "You don't attend a meeting without your planner."

# Reviewing Your Road Warriors

**Y**ou have a library of employee-evaluation material for your in-house staff. But how do you review the performance of your telecommuting salespeople? Carolyn B. Thompson, president of Training Systems, a $280,000 provider of customized training and human-resources consulting in Frankfort, Ill., suggests these steps for **designing your own evaluation system for telecommuters and field sales staff**:

1. Draw up a list of reasonable expectations, benchmarks, and a tentative schedule of "check-in" times that you and the employee agree on.

2. With the help of those benchmarks—such as monthly sales reports—figure out whether the person has met expectations by comparing this year's stats with last year's.

3. Given this year's information, you and the employee should establish measurable goals for the coming year.

4. Finally, ask the employee to write an action plan for achieving those goals. The review system should be "ongoing and participatory," says Thompson.

When scheduling check-ins and reviews, consider how well-linked your telecommuters are to headquarters. In some cases, frequent interaction can mean less frequent reviews.

# 232
**IDEA**

## Murphy's Form Beats Murphy's Law

**W**ith rapid expansion stressing every joint in the company's operation, the last thing anyone at Collectech Systems had time to worry about was paperwork. Bent on opening seven branch offices and topping $5 million in revenues a few years ago, the $11-million accounts-receivable management company in Calabasas, Calif., was dispatching salespeople to new territories in Dallas, Denver, Atlanta, and elsewhere once every six weeks. Of course, as the organization spread out, even trivial administrative tasks became logistical nightmares. Then an employee—serendipitously named Chris Murphy—invented an **electronic expense-reimbursement form**.

Murphy's form, which is just a spreadsheet wearing a little makeup, handles all the computations automatically. Word got out that Murphy's hard drive harbored a solution to the reimbursement rodeo. He e-mailed copies to comrades around the country, and it has since become standard operating procedure for field personnel.

By moving things electronically, Collectech has shaved two weeks off the reimbursement process. But it can't dispense with paper records. "We still need receipts," says controller Gary Palatas. "The IRS, should it ever decide to audit, as well as the CPAs who sign off on our financial statements, require us to back up every expense with a receipt." So accounting won't mail the check until hard copy and receipts arrive at the California headquarters. No problem, Murphy says. "I carry around an envelope, and as I incur expenses, I slip the receipts into that envelope and then mail it off with a printout of the e-mailed report."

**233**

**IDEA**

# "Instant" Payback

**T**ravel-and-entertainment reimbursement had always been a hassle for Sales Mark, a sales-rep firm in Little Rock with $45 million in revenues. "Our 100 salespeople were scattered across 40 states, and reimbursing their monthly expenses used to take about three weeks," recalls Jim Morgan, the company's vice-president of financial reporting. "Since most of these people were younger and didn't have big bank accounts, they couldn't wait that long. So we were always having to give them cash advances that we'd then have to keep track of, too."

Then Sales Mark's managers decided to hire Gelco Information Network, a service provider based in Eden Prairie, Minn., that handles outsourced financial functions. "By **outsourcing T&E reimbursement**, we cut the cycle to three days," Morgan says.

For companies that are considering outsourcing, T&E is a natural starting point. At most companies, the process of T&E reimbursement takes about 17 sequential steps and three weeks or longer. Gelco's process—typical of T&E service providers—takes three business days, from day one (when employees call an 800 number and use the touch-tone keypad to enter their categories of expenses) to the date when funds are electronically transferred into their bank or charge-card accounts. Gelco claims that companies spend $15 to $30 per transaction when they handle T&E internally, while an outsourced T&E transaction can cost as little as $8.

There's one more advantage to outsourced T&E functions: audit control. Gelco's computer automatically verifies that each caller is employed and authorized to receive that level of reimbursement.

# 234
**IDEA**

# Plastic Containers

**E**ntrepreneurs and salespeople entertaining prospects and clients rely heavily on credit cards to get through the week. But a high cost comes with the convenience of plastic. Here are a few guidelines to help you and your sales staff **control credit-card expenses**.

᠔ *Don't use the same card for personal and business purchases.* "Business owners are allowed to deduct credit-card interest on business purchases, but consumers can't deduct personal interest charges," explains Richard M. Colombik, a lawyer and CPA in Schaumburg, Ill. Plus, using the same card blurs the line between business and personal expenses. The IRS may decide those Super Bowl tickets were a personal expense and refuse to let you deduct them. If you can't get a corporate card, get two personal cards and reserve one strictly for business.

᠔ *Shop around for the most realistic deal.* It's not enough to try to get the highest possible credit limit. If you're typically late on several payments each year, shop around for lower late fees as well as low interest rates.

᠔ *Document, document.* Travel and entertainment expenses are a favorite IRS target. Make it a practice to jot down the who, what, and why of a business lunch while you have your pen out to sign the bill, then tuck it away in a regular spot reserved for T&E receipts. "I can't tell you how much money and time business owners waste when they—or their CPAs or lawyers—have to hunt through old records to try to figure out what a credit-card charge was for," comments Harvey J. Berger, an associate partner at Grant Thornton, in the accounting firm's Washington, D.C., office.

# Greens Fees for Uncle Sam?

**D**o you sometimes worry about how much your outside sales staff spends on the road—and how to document those expenses? Travel and entertainment costs are among the most likely targets for the IRS during an audit. To **avoid T&E tax troubles**, Rich Miller, vice-president of small-business travel at American Express, recommends these precautions:

❧ *Make sure employees keep adequate records.* Require employees to record, on original charge receipts, whom they're entertaining and why, so you'll have extra documentation when credit-card issuers send you monthly receipt copies.

❧ *Verify T&E tax records against quarterly statements.* This should help the company pick up tax-deductible charges employees may have forgotten about, as well as incorrectly filed expense charges.

❧ *Require receipts for all expenses over $10.* Setting a receipt minimum lower than the $25 that is required by the IRS will beef up your company's documentation during tax audits.

"To succeed these days, you've got to get better and better at tracking what customers want. In the past, there was competition between great, average, and bad companies. But the bad and the average are being eliminated, leaving only top-notch companies that are more likely to have what the customer wants."

**ROGER D. BLACKWELL**
professor of marketing, Ohio State University,
Columbus, Ohio

# Make No Mistake

Inaccurate data entry can be costly. Without accurate data, orders can't be filled correctly and market forecasting can run amok. At Isis Pharmaceuticals, a $26-million drug development company in Carlsbad, Calif., database records are routinely reviewed by the Food and Drug Administration, which could bring operations to a halt if a few figures are entered incorrectly. So Isis adheres religiously to **a total quality system for data entry** that keeps the database as accurate as possible. Here are the five steps in the process.

1. *Manual review*. Clinical-data coordinator checks entry manually for obvious mistakes.

2. *Double entry*. Once an individual's information has been punched into the database, a second data-entry operator reenters the same information in a new file. The computer then automatically compares the two files and prints out a list of inconsistencies, which must be reconciled by the clinical-data coordinator.

3. *Visual verification*. A data manager compares the data that were entered against the original handwritten forms.

4. *Electronic verification*. A data manager runs a series of relational edit-check programs that examine data in selected fields within the database to make sure they are logical and consistent.

5. *Final audit*. Once an entire clinical trial is completed, Stuart Nixon, director of clinical-data management and biostatistics, and his team conduct one final audit by checking a representative cross-section of data against the original handwritten forms.

# 237
**IDEA**

## Taming the Data Beast

**D**atabases enable a company to follow customer needs, market trends, suppliers' prices, costs, and—oh yes, sales patterns. Still, they need to be properly managed, or they can grow unwieldy. Here's how you can **keep your database under control**.

ᐳ *Be choosy about the information you track.* Clients sometimes ask Lon Orenstein, president of support4u.inc, in Dallas, to track details that aren't worth remembering, like a customer's fraternity membership or his favorite color boxer shorts. It doesn't pay off, and maintenance is costly and a nuisance.

ᐳ *Develop a simple rating system.* You must be able to tell at a glance how important each customer is to your company. Bob Dorf of Marketing1to1/Peppers and Rogers Group, in Stamford, Conn., suggests assigning each customer a score on several variables such as past sales, potential sales, and referrals. You can rank leads the same way.

ᐳ *Keep your list clean.* Make sure company names are entered consistently—use the same form each time. And check the work of temps doing data entry.

ᐳ *Be realistic.* If you can't get people to enter information regularly, the database won't be of much use. One computer-shy executive relays messages about customers to a dedicated voice-mail box; later, an assistant transcribes them and enters the information on the computer.

**238**

IDEA

# If You Build It, They Will Come

**T**ime and again, companies report that once a database is up and running, sales grow at least 10% to 30% as a result. But you can't exactly create one at the snap of a finger. What to do? **Delegate building the database to an unencumbered new employee or farm it out to an independent contractor.**

Case in point: At Dia, a high-fashion sweater company based in Vergennes, Vt., sales reached $1 million in 1995 and stalled. So when the founders hired John Leehman as CEO to move Dia to the next level, he worked with a software consultant for six months to design the company's database. Leehman estimates the cost of the database at a mere $5,000—including the consultant's time.

Using the database, he identified 5 independent sales representatives (out of 11) who were really growing the business. By giving them additional data about their respective territories, the database enabled them to increase their sales by an average of 50%. This propelled the company to more than $4 million in sales in 1997. "This database," says Leehman, "has been the single biggest contributor to the company's growth."

**239**
**IDEA**

# Swords into Plowshares

**U**ntil 1995, former U.S. Marine Dan Caulfield's management style was, well, militaristic. Intensive training sessions, detailed manuals of job instructions, and daily full-staff meetings at 8 a.m. and 5 p.m. to monitor progress helped build sales at Hire Quality, his Chicago-based job placement firm, to more than $1 million in two years.

"I barely had time to think, yet I was unilaterally making all the decisions," says Caulfield. Then, six months after he promoted a staffer to sales manager, revenues took a nosedive. When Caulfield insisted on more cold calls, he discovered that ordering people around didn't necessarily get results. Sales plummeted, and his new sales manager resigned.

In desperation, Caulfield tried **managing sales data instead of salespeople**. He gathered every invoice the company ever sent and began tracking sales closed from cold calls, sales closed from clients calling the company, descriptions of the best contracts, and how the company had gotten those contracts. The graphs couldn't have been clearer: When prospects called the company, sales were closed 79% of the time. Cold calling *wasn't* the answer, after all. Improving marketing efforts to attract high-quality customers brought sales up to $3.3 million in 1997.

Says a humbled Caulfield, "I know now that the way to lead people is to manage information well. Instead of telling employees what to do, I give them objectives and have opened up the company's books so they can make good decisions."

# Staying on Top

In today's volatile marketplace, it may be too late to salvage a downturn if you rely solely on income statements. "The decline of a best-seller and its contribution to your bottom line can be almost instantaneous," warns consultant Max Carey, founder of Corporate Resources Development, a $5-million sales and marketing consultancy in Atlanta. "You've got to watch for it carefully." **To find out whether your company is on top of its most profitable customers, check the following indicators:**

   *Face-to-face meetings.* If customers start keeping their distance, it means they see you as just another bid. Instead of mailing in your best shot, Carey advises, tell them, "We'd love to quote your business, but we don't know enough. We'd rather give you no solution than an incomplete solution." With luck, it will lead to a wider-ranging interaction—and you'll find out where you stand.

   *Unbundled services.* Say you've set a price that includes follow-up, maintenance, 24-hour delivery, and a per-unit cost. Well, the customer says, how much for the item without the quick delivery? "What they are trying to do is reduce the illusion of the sale. They want to strip it down and see what you really think the product is worth," says Carey. That puts you in a no-win situation, and it's another way of keeping the transaction at arm's length. Rethinking your price structure may help to rectify the situation.

   *Price objections.* If your salespeople are down to asking, "What's it going to take to get your business today?" then they're suggesting that the product doesn't have any worth. It's not the customer's job to care about your margins. Make sure you can justify prices by communicating other benefits to be gained from the purchase.

**241**
**IDEA**

# Software for Hard Data

**Y**our company need not break the bank to build a database, since simplicity can be a key to its success.

At USF Seko Worldwide, in Elk Grove Village, Ill., the process of building a marketing database started quietly enough. The freight forwarder's marketing vice-president bought a copy of ACT! software and began playing with it on his laptop. Soon, what had started as an experiment turned into an essential tool for most of the company's sales reps. Reps now come to appointments loaded with routing information and historical sales data—what, where, how often, and how much a customer ships. Even though Seko is a fairly big company—its sales have climbed to around $106 million—it has found that an **inexpensive contact-management program** like ACT! can satisfy the company's need for a marketing database.

Although contact managers are often thought of as the poor man's solution to sales-force automation, programs such as GoldMine, Maximizer, Sharkware, Microsoft Outlook, and ACT! can be used to build a fairly potent database, at prices starting at about $99 for a single user and $650 for a five-user network license. Their implicit promise: Anyone can turn a knack for networking into hard sales.

# Fancy Footwork

In the summer of 1994, Mike and Brendan Moylan, co-owners of Sports Endeavors, in Hillsborough, N.C., saw one shoe drop—and another, and another, and another. One of the buyers for their mail-order company purchased 30,000 pairs of soccer shoes, expecting them to sell within two months. But by September, about 15,000 pairs were still languishing in the stockroom. "It was our summer of enlightenment," says Mike. The brothers decided to install a **database marketing system to analyze sales trends and facilitate smarter purchasing decisions**.

They ended up two years later with a data-warehousing program loaded onto a Data General Aviion minicomputer and eight 486 PCs. Now, every Saturday, Sports Endeavors' techies update their Cognos (613-738-1440) program with the week's purchasing information. Buyers can click on a vendor's name and, within seconds, see a range of data pertaining to it, or they can funnel down further to see how well the vendor's cleats sold during the past few months. Expecting a slow beginning, the Moylans decided to focus first on forecasting. Example: Analyzing a 20% growth in sales of adidas watches in 1995 enabled the company's four buyers to build a month-by-month sales plan for 1996.

# The ABCs of Activity-Based Costing

**T**wenty percent of a company's customers account for 200% of its profit, according to Professor Bala Balachandran of Northwestern University's Kellogg Graduate School of Management. "The remaining 80% actually lose money," he says, "which is how companies end up with their final 100%." A company loses money on sales for a variety of reasons. Small orders, back orders for out-of-stock products, requests for special handling, late payments after repeated follow-ups, demands for returns, and the like all eat into the profit margins of a sale. Most companies have no clue how much they spend on meeting those demands, so they can't factor them into their pricing.

To get a grip on your company's costs so that you can issue more profitable price quotes, you may want to take a lesson from companies that have turned to **activity-based costing (ABC) software packages to track bids on jobs more accurately**.

Several companies make software products that facilitate the ABC process, including EasyABC Plus (503-617-7100), HyperABC (404-842-7777), and NetProphet (905-678-1661). For about $10,000, you can get software and enough vendor-supplied training to get your system up and running. Most companies bring in consultants to help customize off-the-shelf ABC software to reflect their specific operations. The investment, users say, is worth it. Within three to six weeks, most start learning which customers are profitable and which ones aren't.

"Half my time as a salesperson is spent helping customers solve problems that relate in no way to my product, and I don't earn a dime doing it. To create a loyal customer, I do everything I can to make sure a customer is satisfied—not just satisfied with my product."

TOM COTTINGHAM
founder, NarrowCast Concepts,
Louisville

**IDEA**

# Formula for Success

**S**ay you're about to roll out a seasonal mail campaign or exhibit at a trade show. What kind of sales payback can you expect from such marketing initiatives? Is there a general rule? M.H. "Mac" McIntosh, president of The Mac McIntosh Co., a $400,000 consulting firm in Redondo Beach, Calif., thinks so.

McIntosh, who tracks sales leads for a living, has developed benchmarks that he says can be used in business-to-business selling scenarios. Through research studies for his customers that traced more than 40,000 sales inquiries, McIntosh has found that 24% of people who respond to a promotion will buy from someone—either you or a competitor—within 6 months. Forty-five percent, he says, will buy within 12 months. "Within a year, nearly one in two will buy somebody's product or service," McIntosh explains. Here's his **formula for projecting a sales promotion's performance**:

*(# of raw leads) x (% who will buy from someone) x (average $ sales amount) x (% you contact) x (% you normally close) = gross-revenue potential*

If you follow up on leads for six months, for example, you'd plug in 0.24 for "percent who will buy from someone." Closing rates vary widely, but whatever your norm is, McIntosh firmly believes it can be bettered by simply following through on the leads sitting in your lap. He finds that companies follow up on only about 10% to 15% of inquiries, on average.

# Where'd We Go Wrong?

**M**ost company owners hate to hear harsh words about their "babies," so the hardest part of tracking lost customers is picking up the phone. To avoid that discomfort, Bob Ottley, president of One Step Tree and LawnCare, in North Chili, N.Y., used an independent consulting firm to conduct One Step's first telephone survey. The firm called active customers as well as those who had canceled the service. The results were sobering: A full 32%, or 719 of 2,250 customers, had defected, and many wouldn't say why.

Now One Step **persistently keeps track of its customer list**, and Ottley acts on the weekly "cancels" report. He's halved the attrition rate, and he knows why customers failed to renew. In the first half of 1994, for example, 19% of nonrenewers had moved, 16% decided to maintain their lawns themselves, 12% could no longer afford the service, and 8% opted for a cheaper competitor. Among the rest, only 4% gave no explanation.

Since 1988, One Step has conducted two more comprehensive surveys, its customer base has doubled, and its revenues have shot up to $1.7 million. "Our leave-behind survey card helped a lot," says Ottley. "It puts the idea into the customer's head that we want to know if there's a problem."

**IDEA**

# Close to Home

**I**nvolvement in local business helped Yantis Corp., a $25-million highway-construction company in San Antonio, survive Texas's real estate bust of the late 1980s.

During the mid-1980s, chairman John Yantis, who served on the board of a local savings and loan, convinced his sons that a slowdown was coming. Preparing for the hard times, president Tom Yantis and executive vice-president Mike Yantis developed a multipronged strategy that their company still relies on. It involves diversification and improved tracking of their market. Instead of specializing only in highly profitable—but cyclical—private-development work, the company has diversified into city, state, and even federal projects.

Now the Yantises **track private real estate projects approved by local planning and zoning boards**—a good indicator of construction activity six months ahead or more. With that information, they can vary their business mix and, with several options to choose from, adjust their company's plans as economic conditions change.

## 247
**IDEA**

# Vintage Salesmeister

**A**gustin Huneeus, president of a $50-million winery in Rutherford, Calif., noticed that when he went to a fancy restaurant to dine, he rarely found one of his own Franciscan Estate Selections wines on the wine list. "Where on earth is my product being sold?" he wondered.

To **take control of where his product went**, Huneeus had to contact 50 distributors, find out which stores, restaurants, hotels, and nightclubs they were selling to, track those sales, and then offer them guidance on how best to change their strategies. He and his son, vice-president of sales Agustin Francisco Huneeus Jr., ended up buying Trade Account Management, a proprietary system developed by MKF Systems (707-963-9222) that was customized to work with GoldMine (GoldMine Software, 800-654-3526), an off-the-shelf contact-management program. Trade Account Management includes a central database on a Micron file server; GoldMine is tied into the system and loaded on salespeople's laptops.

Here's how it works: Distributors send their reports to the database electronically. Trade Account Management breaks out the sales numbers and dates from each distributor's accounts and arranges them by region, state, zip code, and type of wine. Huneeus can then mine the system for intelligence, such as how his Chardonnays sold in 1992 or how his Cabernets did in the Midwest. GoldMine, on the other hand, houses the demographic information. By dialing into the Micron file server, salespeople can retrieve or send updated demographic information whenever they need to.

Plans are now under way to integrate contact management functions into the Trade Account Management software, eliminating the need for two programs.

## 248
### IDEA

# The Eye Is Quicker Than the Machine

**S**ales tracking can be as simple as listening to the people in the shipping department who see what's really happening. Long before the accounting department gets around to entering figures on the computer and analyzing the data, employees who deal directly with orders see what's selling and what's not.

On Friday afternoons, Deborah Williams, owner and CEO of Black Cat Computer Wholesale, in Amherst, N.Y., holds a **Q&A session to find out what employees are thinking**—wherever they happen to be working. These informal sessions pay off: A shipping clerk, for example, noticed that the sales of one product seemed to be lagging when he was checking orders going out the door. The insight prompted Williams to lower prices, boosting sales by 7%. "It's something that just dropped through the cracks," she says. "It was just a little piece of what we sell, but now it's an important chunk of our business." That fellow from shipping is now a manager at Black Cat.

## Proof Positive

Janet J. Kraus and Kathy Sherbrooke, cofounders of Circles, a Boston-based five-person start-up that provides personal convenience services, have a unique method for checking that their employees are maintaining good written records of the company's 1,100 customers. Every week, Circles' employees **swap customer files** with one another and review them to see if they contain adequate and appropriate information. Kraus also checks some files herself.

The benchmark: Could someone randomly call another rep's customer and provide good service without missing a beat? If the answer is uncertain, the rep makes the call to test a file's usefulness.

**IDEA**

# The Rating Game

**C**ampbell Software, a fast-growing *Inc.* 500 company in Chicago that sells a workforce-management package used by such big retailers as the Gap, appeared to have unlimited potential. There was just one hitch: No one had any real idea how many of the stacks of qualified prospects would turn into sales—or when. The only thing that newly arrived sales vice-president Tom Colby could tell for sure was that the sales cycle would often grind on for up to 12 months.

Colby adopted the approach described in a book entitled *Solution Selling: Creating Buyers in Different Selling Markets*, by Michael T. Bosworth (McGraw-Hill, 800-262-7429, 1995, $27.50): **an A-B-C-D rating system to make sure salespeople forecast accurately**. If a salesperson has met with the prospective client, thinks there's a good match, and has confirmed that a budget exists, the prospect is graded D, indicating a 20% chance of becoming a sale. A C grade (30% chance of a sale) indicates that the salesperson has met several executives with decision-making power, conducted a needs analysis, and discussed a theoretical timetable for the sale. "A grade of B," says Colby, "is troubling. It means we've gone through the whole process and we should get a contract but, for reasons unknown to us, they decide they can't do it now." Campbell eliminates Bs from the immediate forecast, since they can clog up the works. Finally, the A level (90% chance of sale) signifies that contract negotiations are under way.

How well does the system work? Campbell has shortened its sales cycle to just six to nine months, doubled its sales each year, and gotten to within 10% of its annual sales targets.

**251**

**IDEA**

# It Must Be the Weather

If you think your business is immune to seasonal weather, you may want to take a closer look at your company's sales history. On the surface, Multiplex, a St. Louis-based manufacturer of automatic beverage-dispensing equipment, is a seasonless supplier, selling restaurant equipment to chains including McDonald's and TGI Friday's. After all, since people eat and drink every day, conventional wisdom says that its business isn't weather-related—but it is.

"We like the summer," says chairman J.W. Kisling. "Equipment starts failing when the weather gets hot. People are thirsty, so they are drinking a lot." And if a restaurant has to turn away thirsty customers because a machine is on the fritz, it's a solid prospect for Multiplex, which provides customers with 24-hour repair service.

Since the company prides itself on providing better service than its competitors, **the season of equipment breakdowns is a perfect time to win new business**. "Our sales representatives go back and call on customers who have said they are satisfied with their current vendor, during the hot summer months when they aren't likely to be so happy." Typically it can take years to close a sale, according to Kisling, so they've used every trick in the book to spur growth. Multiplex is now a $34-million company.

**252**
**IDEA**

# Dear Diary

Once a company has a history of sales, it may need a database to track them. But as Jane Wesman discovered, a simple notebook may do the trick for tracking general trends. As head of Jane Wesman Public Relations, in New York City, Wesman **keeps a business journal at home to record her personal reactions** and never brings it with her to the office, where someone might be tempted to read it. The diary helps her run her business better because, by rereading it, she can detect trends that would otherwise be missed.

"For example," says Wesman, "my business journal helped me realize that it's almost impossible for me to close sales around Christmas. Until I recognized this pattern from several years' worth of journals, I grew anxious every year when business slowed near the holidays. Now I can stop worrying about that normal seasonal dip and prepare for it instead."

**253**

**IDEA**

# Onward Spiral

In an age of high-tech communication gadgets and productivity tools, there's still one decidedly low-tech item that many wired executives swear by: ye olde spiral notebook.

Karen Settle, president and CEO of $5-million Keystone Marketing Specialists, in Las Vegas, **carries her notebook wherever she goes**, entering running notes from client meetings and a phone log as she works her way through the day.

Settle says the notebook serves two purposes. First, it captures everything chronologically in simple diary fashion. Second, it discourages her from scribbling notes and phone numbers on stray pieces of paper—a sure ticket to business hell. When she calls on new accounts—a time when first impressions matter—Settle takes notes on a pad inside a leather-bound portfolio and staples the pages into her notebook later.

She talks about replacing her notebook with a handheld personal digital assistant, which would function as her address book and a link to her office e-mail (she rarely lugs a laptop when she travels). But taking notes on the tiny keyboard might be too awkward for client meetings.

Settle fills a notebook every month or so. By the end it looks a little ratty, but it still does the job. As a side benefit, it's also a helpful reference for legal matters and IRS audits.

# X

"A selling process that's inefficient or broken doesn't disappear by adding technology. But integration of technology often includes closer scrutiny of the process. It gives business owners a chance to put checks and balances in place, which was simply not possible with a manual system or older technology."

**BILL GATES**
founder and CEO, Microsoft Corp.,
Redmond, Wash.

# 254
**IDEA**

## Net Your Customers

**B**efore he makes sales calls, Doug Wright, president of a $4-million New York City graphic-design firm, prepares a Web page for his prospects. Customers can see from the very start how effectively they will be kept up-to-date on every aspect of their relationships with Wright.

You, too, can feed your relationship with your clientele by sending news about your company—such as new hires, works-in-progress, company expansions, and other relevant information—over the Web. A **customized, password-protected Web page for each customer or client** is key to making all of them feel special.

Wright Communications also uses the Web for project tracking. Its password-protected sites enable clients to view work in progress, approve changes, or sign off on finished work by e-mail. Wright can set up a new client page in less than half an hour. Having Web pages for its customers "positions us as a leader and innovator in the field," says Wright.

# 255
**IDEA**

## Everybody Get Animated

How can your Internet customers know what they're buying if they can only see a picture of it on a little computer screen? The next best thing to going to the mall would be to examine a three-dimensional, moveable product right at home. But shoppers don't want to wait for slow-moving Internet video—they need a product image that can fit easily and quickly through a 28.8 Kbps modem.

The technology that allows companies to do this is animation. Because animated imagery, unlike video, can be made machine-readable, it requires less bandwidth and is much quicker to download. Animation is also more flexible than video, because every aspect of the medium can be controlled by the user.

Companies like Myski, in Los Altos, Calif., **use animation to give customers control over design and an accurate image** of what they're going to buy. Consumers clicking on its Web site (www.myski.com) can design their own skis (colors, logos, text) and then rotate the finished design to see how the skis look before the company's eight employees custom-make them. "Animation is the closest we can get to hands-on through the Internet channel," says company president Chris Jorgensen.

# 256
**IDEA**

## Not Just Idle Chat

**L**ike many small and midsize companies, TC Computers, a systems and upgrade operation in Jefferson, La., has been **providing customer-service functions online**. Instead of talking customers through problems, reps do it using ConferenceRoom by WebMaster (www.webmaster.com, 408-345-1800). "What we really like is that you can float the chat interface and keep it with you while you look through other pages," says TC president Darin Oreman. This allows the technical-support person and the perplexed customer to look at the same file while typing their online discussion in a corner of the screen. The only drawback, notes Oreman, is that the Web-site chat room is open 24 hours a day, seven days a week, so someone must be available at all times to respond to customers.

Prospects as well as customers are dropping by the chat room. One of the greatest features of ConferenceRoom, according to Oreman, is the ability to continue chatting while "traveling" outside TC's site (www.tccomputers.com), even to a competitor's site. "We assume that anyone looking at our site is looking at 10 others," says Oreman. "If they carry our chat room with them, then they are likely to ask us—not our competitor—if they have questions." That ability to interact easily and informally with TC reps has made closing sales easier.

# 257
**IDEA**

## Virtually Persuasive

On the Web, in-depth information is a powerful and persuasive sales tool. It also helps to overcome a major inhibitor of Internet commerce: a simple lack of trust in the vendors themselves.

Robert Olson and Peter Granoff, creators of an Internet wine store called Virtual Vineyards (www.virtualvin.com), based in Palo Alto, Calif., have been tackling that particular problem by **giving lots of concrete product information and reviving the personal touch** that has nearly disappeared with the rise of the superstore. By doing so, they have managed to establish credibility in a niche market.

Granoff, a wine maven with a good reputation in the San Francisco Bay Area, offers advice on topics such as wineglass selection and the relation of storage methods to climate. He also instructs users on taste and the operating details of specific producers. Olson works on making the Web site even more personal and intimate. For example, he can use customers' own preferences, gleaned from their order histories, to present wine options in line with their previous orders. "Every time we strengthen the authorial presence, people respond," says Olson.

# The Farther, the Better

**W**onderful as Web sites are, they aren't cheap to create. One way to lower the price for **Web-site design is to farm it out—way out—to a designer outside the United States**. Companies that need a Web page have discovered overseas providers whose prices are much lower than those of American firms.

Tropical Jim's Remake Shop, a Web-design firm with revenues of $373,500, based in Caracas, Venezuela, is an example. "Ninety percent of our customers are Americans, partly because salaries in this country are 10% of U.S. salaries for equivalent work," says owner Jim Macintyre. "We've doubled our size and plan to do so again in 1998."

When Web surfers see something they like, they simply buy it. "Many visitors do not seem to care, or do not stop to think about, where on the planet you are based," adds another Web-site designer, in England.

**259**

**IDEA**

# Small Space, Cosmic Possibilities

**M**any an entrepreneur working out of a home office or cramped commercial quarters dreads questions like, "Let me come out to your place" and "Can I see your client list?" Fear not. The business universe is expanding. Thanks to the great equalizer—technology—you can **do all your promotions on the Internet**. In cyberspace, no one can see how small your corporate headquarters are—and targeted marketing campaigns can succeed without a big budget.

Image Soup, a $2-million multimedia consultancy in St. Louis, generates 40% of its qualified sales leads by broadcasting a monthly newsletter by e-mail or fax to 250 customer contacts and to another 2,500 prospects who have attended an Image Soup seminar, inquired about a product, or were referred to the company by a vendor.

# 260
**IDEA**

## The Little Engine That Could

If you have a Web site, search engines are key to increasing the number of hits you get. But how do you get on search engines? How do you get your site to come out high on the list when someone does a search? Should you put a hot topic's catch phrase in the text to get more hits?

Before you get carried away with quadratic equations and buzzwords, you might want to try a new product called WebPosition Agent (I.S.T., $99 to $289, 800-962-4855, www.webposition.com). The **program monitors your site's ranking on all the top search engines**, including AltaVista, Yahoo!, and Excite.

Let's say you have a Web site that sells baseball cards. You can type in words like baseball, Babe Ruth, and Dodgers, and the WebPosition software will go out and bring you a detailed report of how your site fared on each engine. You can even set the program to automatically check your site's position—or your competitor's position—daily, weekly, or monthly.

If you discover that your site falls at the bottom of the engines' lists, don't despair. WebPosition Agent offers tips on how to boost your ranking. It might tell you, for example, to use the plural form of words on your site rather than the singular, so that people searching under either form—say *card* or *cards*—will pick it up. The folks at I.S.T. also send out a newsletter via e-mail with updates on the best ways to use search engines.

# 261
## IDEA

# Serving Up Sales

**W**hen SoftPro Books, a computer-book retailer in Burlington, Mass., decided to add another "location" by creating a virtual store through a cybermall, it hit a snag: SoftPro failed to consider the importance of flexibility in managing and updating a site that deals with a fast-changing topic such as technology. After a year of operation, the site had drawn little more than an occasional sale. "Titles go in and out of fashion in weeks, not years," says Bob Treitman, vice-president of finance and operations for the 10-person company. Whenever he wanted to make a change to the site, Treitman used to have to call the cybermall's Webmaster, which meant days of waiting.

Then Treitman got a **server that could be accessed from any Web browser** so that he could make changes or retrieve order information himself using his password. Treitman can also get reports about the sites his customers come from, which helps him plan strategic partnerships. Web sales now account for 5% of SoftPro's revenues—up from virtually nil a year earlier.

# Make Your Database Earn Its Keep

Is your company's database a hot Web site waiting to happen? Here's how Powell's Bookstores turned its inventory tracking system into a selling tool. Historically, bookseller Michael Powell's competitive advantage has been his company's wide selection—about 500,000 titles in stock on an average day. Computerizing this mammoth mountain of data was one of the more torturous processes Powell has been through. In addition to inventory, Powell's Bookstores buys 2,000 to 4,000 used titles daily. The company had to get custom software to control the constantly changing database; then, it took one year of steady drudgery for data entry.

As soon as the scutwork was done, the next logical step was to **take the digital information online**. The company, based in Portland, Ore., made its Internet debut in 1993. Within hours the virtual bookstore was receiving orders. Since going online, sales have grown by 10% to 20% a month. By 2002, says Powell, the store may bring in a third of its sales online. Already, Powell's Bookstores employs 360 people and has sales of more than $30 million.

# 263
**IDEA**

## Going Once, Going Twice

**A**t conventional Web stores with fixed prices, buyers place orders by filling out forms—a humdrum experience at best. Buyers and sellers in an online auction, however, become part of a community—chatting, sharing experiences, and even arranging private trades. And bidding, which is by definition a kind of contest, offers an exciting way to shop online.

Traditionally, sellers of surplus goods post descriptions to appropriate groups, and prospective buyers give return bids via e-mail. The chief problem with that system is that bidders can't always see what the competition is offering.

Pierre Omidyar, CEO and founder of eBay, in San Jose, Calif., dared to dream of a more automated and socially fulfilling method. His eBay **online auction software posts how much participants are willing to pay**, so that buyers can place bids accordingly.

Business is booming (10 million transactions since 1995) and self-promoting. The site's creators soon learned that sellers posting descriptions of their items at other locations on the Internet would embed links in their messages; buyers clicking on those links were delivered right to the seller's page on eBay. From there, the buyers frequently wandered to other auctions at the site—generating more business and, by extension, publicity for eBay's site.

**264**
**IDEA**

# Get Yourself on the E-List

**M**ining the Internet for sales leads has been notoriously iffy. Now, leading publishers of business-to-business information are going digital with **sophisticated databases that make online commerce more efficient**.

General Electric Information Services, a global electronic-commerce company, and Thomas Publishers, which produces the *Thomas Register of American Manufacturers*, launched an online company called TPN Register (www.tpnregister.com). Headquartered in Washington, D.C., TPN Register uses line-item detail and product headings similar to those in hardcover reference books to facilitate the buying and selling process.

Perhaps the most ambitious online trade service is Unibex, which offers one-stop shopping for the full range of trade services. The U.S. Chamber of Commerce (www.uschamber.org) is so enthusiastic about the system that it sells memberships at discounted rates to its 215,000 members. At this site, the shopper fills out a questionnaire to create a detailed request. When the entire bid has been defined, the server searches for matching offers. If any are found, the parties negotiate by revising one another's offers, using the site's menu sequences.

Robert Wan of Master System, a sporting goods distributor based in Arcadia, Calif., used the system to source hiking boots from Canadian manufacturers, which have an excellent reputation. In the old days, finding a bootmaker in Canada required attending trade shows or pawing through directories of manufacturers. He would then have to play a lengthy game of telephone tag. With Unibex, he sourced a Canadian supplier in less than a day.

**265**

IDEA

# Is It EDI or Else?

**R**eady or not, the age of electronic partnering has arrived. For many small businesses, that will mean replacing conventional order-taking and invoicing with electronic data interchange (EDI), which hooks computers together via telephone lines to swap information. Large retailers, manufacturers, and the U.S. government are pushing EDI hard because they can save millions of dollars processing orders.

Being prepared can make the difference between being a coveted electronic partner and being an EDI casualty. Here are **three tips for going EDI**:

1. *Don't wait*. Talk to customers, and see what others in your industry are doing. Don't be caught off guard with a letter from a customer that says it's either EDI or good-bye.

2. *Get help*. If you're having trouble figuring out how to go online, consider hiring a consultant. The EDI World Institute (514-288-3555) can point you to a consultant in your area. Several publications can help you learn more about EDI: *The Why EDI Guide for Small- and Medium-sized Enterprises* and *EDI Window* (514-288-3555), *EDI Forum: The Journal of Electronic Commerce* (708-848-0135), and *EDI News* (301-424-3338). To go online with the federal government, contact the Federal Electronic Commerce Acquisition Program Management Office (703-681-0364/9) and the Department of Defense Electronic Commerce Information Center (800-EDI-3414).

3. *Leverage your EDI investment*. Once you're online with one customer, adding others shouldn't be difficult or expensive. And EDI capability will help you attract new business.

# 266
### IDEA

# Safer E-Shopping

The easier your business makes it for customers to hand over their money, the more sales you'll achieve. And now it's getting easier for shoppers to spend via the Web, too. Consumers wary of computer technology and its risks are being reassured by the use of **new security products that make online transactions as safe as money in the bank**. By 2003, according to Forrester Research, in Cambridge, Mass., revenue from online shopping is expected to balloon from $518 million to $6.6 billion.

To get in on the ground floor of this sales explosion, equip your Web site with software embedded with secure sockets layer (SSL), which scrambles credit-card numbers and other electronic data so that they're useless to unauthorized recipients. Another, even more secure option is to build out your Web site with secure electronic transaction (SET). This system skips the retailer, sending the scrambled data straight to a bank, where the information is decoded and the transaction is approved. SET is a boon to retailers because it clears credit-card transactions quickly.

Both SSL and SET require server software. Microsoft's Internet Information Server 3.0 is free, while Netscape's Enterprise Server 2.01 sells for $1,295. An advantage of Netscape's system is that it supports both Unix and Windows NT; Microsoft's product does not. If your Web site isn't equipped for SSL, you can retrofit it with a product like SecureWeb Toolkit, from Terisa Systems, in Los Altos, Calif. The Computer Security Institute, in San Francisco (415-905-2626), can refer you to security experts who can help you install the server software, as can resellers and systems integrators.

# 267
**IDEA**

# Translate Queries into Sales

James Kantor is a little embarrassed. The CEO of Eastern Avionics International, a $6-million company that markets navigation and communications equipment to private pilots, admits that he used to delete e-mail from overseas prospects, for the simple reason that he can only read English.

The company, based in Punta Gorda, Fla., often receives e-mail in foreign languages. So when Kantor would find such an e-mail, he'd either ignore it or send a standard reply asking for an English translation. He'd often never hear from the prospect again. He considered hiring bilingual salespeople, but the pickings in southwestern Florida were slim.

Then his Web-site developer introduced him to Comprende, **an Internet-based service that translates e-mail, Web pages, and online chats and newsgroups** into French, Spanish, German, Italian, and Portuguese (Globalink, www.comprende.globalink.com, $250 setup plus $100 a month for a corporate account). Now when Kantor gets a foreign e-mail, he copies the message into a box on the Comprende Web site, types Eastern Avionics' e-mail address into the "sender" and "receiver" lines, selects the language to translate, and submits it. Within a minute or so, Kantor receives an e-mail from Comprende's server with an English translation.

Comprende is not without its flaws. Translations of idiomatic phrases can be humorously literal, and words that the software doesn't understand remain in the original language. Kantor, however, discovered what his company had been missing by not reading all its e-mail. In the first 10 weeks he used Comprende, international sales increased by 60%. "Our average sale ticket is well over $1,000," Kantor says.

**268**

IDEA

# Spam-Free Cyber Promos

**O**n the Internet, unrequested e-mail promoting a product or service—a.k.a. spam—is a lot less effective than traditional direct mail. Netizens don't like spam (the electronic equivalent of junk mail) and are more likely to respond by "flaming" you than buying your product. But there is another approach proving effective in some early tests: opt-in e-mail.

"On the Internet, it really has to be opt-in, otherwise you'll annoy a lot of people and your response rate isn't going to be very high," says Rosalind Resnick, president of NetCreations, a large opt-in e-mail list manager in New York City.

NetCreations and its counterparts compile **lists of Internet users who voluntarily request information** about certain products or product categories. While the lists are small compared to traditional direct-mail lists (NetCreations, with 700,000 unique names, is considered the largest), they can be effective. The consumer response rate to NetCreations' opt-in e-mail messages is 7% to 10%, reports Resnick. The typical response to spam advertising is less than 1%.

However, this response rate comes at a price: While you can rent direct-mail lists for around $100 per thousand names, opt-in e-mail lists cost from $150 to $300 per thousand (including delivery).

Companies that might not be ready to test opt-in e-mail to outside lists might start by testing their own lists. For example, NetCreations recently began delivering e-mail for J. Crew to 750,000 people who had registered their names at the cataloger's Web site.

**269**

IDEA

# Correspondence School

**S**alespeople have always been notorious telephone addicts. Now they are getting hooked on e-mail, too. While e-mail is wonderful for keeping clients posted on projects and communicating with in-house sales personnel, it can also be an unproductive drain on your time. That's why Karen Settle, president and CEO of Keystone Marketing Specialists, a $5-million marketing company in Las Vegas, devised a strategy to avoid scrolling through junk mail and unimportant messages.

Settle has created **an e-mail subaccount, analogous to an unlisted telephone number, and gives the address out sparingly**. Knowing that important e-mail comes into that account, she checks it first. An assistant monitors her general account, which Settle peruses herself when there's time. She says the information influx is worth it because it allows her to nurture relationships with clients and employees.

Other ways to manage e-mail overload:

❧ Assign messages priority rankings for internal communications to flag their importance. Your software probably came with rankings (e.g., priority, urgent, etc.) that you can assign to each message.

❧ Stipulate that employees list action items at the top of the message.

❧ Refuse the temptation to reply to copies of messages. That way you can supervise managers to whom you've delegated control by checking in with them later.

# 270
**IDEA**

## Clip Desk

**D**o you regularly need information about a customer's industry? Or are you simply overwhelmed by the tremendous amount of market data on the Internet? You can effortlessly collect news that's germane to your company and customer base by **subscribing to a personal news delivery service** such as PointCast (www.pointcast.com), My Yahoo! (edit.my.yahoo.com), or NewsPage (www.newspage.com). With these services, the information is automatically sent to you. You only get the information you request when you register for the service, so it's like having a personal clipping service.

Although "push technology," as it's called, is less able to discern good from bad than an old-fashioned human being, it's certainly a whole lot easier and faster than wading through irrelevant postings.

# 271
**IDEA**

## Get Their Number

**Y**ou've got a much better chance of making a sale on the Internet if you can speak directly to the potential customer. Internet inquiries are less serious than telephone inquiries, so it's a good idea to **ask cybervisitors for a phone number**.

India Hatch, owner of Taos Valley Resort Association, a central-booking operation for northern New Mexico that does $7 million in reservations a year, does just that: She hooks prospects over the Internet, then reels them in by talking to them. Hatch estimates that 10% of the inquiries she's gotten through her Web site have converted to actual reservations, while other visitors still balk at giving out their phone numbers.

Hatch's technique isn't profitable yet, but "we'd be foolish not to be on the Internet," given its growth potential, she says. "If we could get 20% conversion, which is a great conversion rate for any central-reservation system, we'd be in the profit mode." Talking to people—humanizing the contact with them—is how she hopes to get there.

# 272
**IDEA**

## Talk Is Cheap, Literally

There are codes your phone company would prefer you didn't know—codes that would give you access to cheaper long-distance carriers that bypass your primary service. "The industry has a dirty little secret," says Robert Pokress, founder and CEO of MediaCom, a manufacturer of PC-based telephone software in Bedford, Mass. "You don't have to be locked into one long-distance company."

Long-distance carriers buy access to the existing telephone infrastructure in bulk at discounted rates and resell it. To take advantage of this peculiar arrangement, Pokress developed the PhoneMiser service (www.phonemiser.com) to **find the cheapest rate for long-distance calls**. The service consists of a software program and a hardware device that plugs into the parallel port of a PC. Each time you dial a long-distance number, PhoneMiser routes the call by using special codes to access the cheapest carrier. The software costs just under $50, but Pokress estimates that it could save small businesses more than 50% on their phone bills.

# Gamma Tester

**G**iven the fast pace of business, a salesperson needs every edge possible when it comes to personal productivity. Take a genuine gadget guy like Steve Ettridge, founder of Temps & Co., a placement agency in Alexandria, Va. His Porsche Carrera is equipped with a plug-in port for faxes and e-mail—as a mobile office for shuttling between headquarters and 15 branches. He steers clear of laptops because they're too short on battery life. Instead, he packs a U.S. Robotics PalmPilot, a Motorola StarTAC cellular phone, and a Motorola text pager. This high-tech trinity helps Ettridge field five dozen phone calls a day, even while out of the office.

Like so many techies, Ettridge is constantly upgrading his mobile productivity tools. How does he keep up with new models, upgrades, and features for all this gear? He doesn't. Instead, his **systems manager serves as a "royal taster," testing new gadgets**. "He gets to buy any productivity tool he wants, and he gives me a briefing on whether it's worth playing with or not," says Ettridge. Whatever doesn't pass muster with his systems manager—20% to 30% of the purchases—can generally be returned for full refunds within 30 days.

Companies lacking an obvious geek to serve as tech-taster need not despair, says Ettridge. If you know any college students, one of them would surely love the job.

# Pick My Minibrain

**N**ame a gadget, and Jeffrey Epstein probably owns it. His business is reselling sales-force automation products, so he has tried most gadgets on the market to help him grow his own company. At the head of the list, at least for the moment, is the Voice Organizer 6200 series **miniature high-tech voice recorders**, palm-sized and shaped like a guitar pick (Voice Powered Technology, 800-255-2310, $99.95 to $149.95). Epstein, CEO of BOSS Systems, in Wilmette, Ill., likes to put one on his desk next to his pager so that he looks like a "gadget guy." The tiny gizmo comes with up to 60 minutes of recording time and holds as many as 200 phone numbers.

"To activate most functions," says Epstein, "I just push a button and speak into the microphone. When I want to retrieve a phone number, first I have to manually select the letter of the alphabet where I stored the number. Then I speak the name, which instantly appears, along with the number, on the liquid crystal display. The recorder also comes in handy for listening to directions as I'm driving to someone's house or office. It's like having a talking notebook wherever I go." The newest version of the Voice Organizer has an optional PC link: After installing the software, you can upload and download information back and forth between the gadget and your computer.

# 275
**IDEA**

## Loaded Messages

**G**reat news: Personal communication tools—pagers, cell phones, and voice mail—are speeding up selling cycles for many small businesses. Not-so-great news: Executives say the tools are making them too accessible.

More and more wired professionals are calling "time out" and setting limits on how much the new technology controls their lives. Take the case of Karen Settle, CEO of Keystone Marketing Specialists, a $5-million company in Las Vegas.

Settle shudders at the thought of trying to run her business without her two favorite tools: an Erikson cellular phone and SkyTel SkyWord pager. "Stand in line to use a pay phone and then, dial 36 numbers to make a call? No way!" But a mobile telephone can wreak havoc on a sales call if it rings at an inopportune moment. That's why she uses the cell phone only for outgoing calls, rarely leaves it on, and **asks clients and employees to leave brief messages on the 800 number of her pager**.

Whenever she's out of the office, Settle clips the pager to her waistband and sets it to "vibrate," not audio. The 240-character limit on messages helps keep them short and sweet, a virtue fast fading from e-mail and voice mail. Settle has equipped all of her key employees with pagers as well. Her sole guideline: If it's a client issue, use the pager. She uses her own pager for additional tasks. If she can't be there in person to give an employee a pat on the back, she leaves a message on his or her pager: "Good job, I like how you handled that."

**276**

IDEA

## Show Time

**D**avid Harris, president of Harris Group, in Kingsport, Tenn., has been adventurous about technology since high tech meant calculators and overhead projectors. Each of the 11 people in his $600,000 insurance and financial-services firm carries an IBM-compatible notebook computer with a color screen. Using graphics packages and dial-in links to mainframes, the salespeople can **instantly demonstrate to prospects how new programs would work for them**—such as a new retirement plan or employee-benefits program.

Harris is a 38-year veteran who is careful to keep his computer investments focused on the top and bottom lines. "We're operating with probably one-sixth the staff we had before," he says. By cutting paperwork and allowing salespeople to run through complex financial scenarios more quickly, use of the notebook computers "has improved our bottom line by probably 20% to 30%." Besides being more efficient, the computers' ability to do real-time analysis gives Harris's people added credibility.

With all that information at their fingertips, the greatest problem is keeping it simple. "You have to train your people not to put out more than the client can absorb at one time," says Harris. In other words, no 100-page reports when two or three pages will do. What's more, it galls Harris to "see some guy trying to draw boxes for two days" instead of selling. So his salespeople use standard formats for reports and presentations. The aim: "To keep salespeople focused on their primary job, which is to sell."

**IDEA**

# Bridging the Gap

**S**hould you automate your sales department? The question begs an answer as laptop-computer prices continue to fall. Nevertheless, stories of companies' agonizing attempts to move from paper to PC can't be ignored, either. According to George W. Colombo, author of *Sales Force Automation: Using the Latest Technology to Make Your Sales Force More Competitive* (McGraw-Hill, 800-722-4726, 1994, $27.95), a little planning prevents disaster:

- *Involve the sales force early.* Give salespeople time to adjust. They're more likely to use the system if they've helped design it and **understand how automation can help their performance**.

- *Use prototypes and trial runs.* Salespeople who aren't computer experts won't know what they want at first. Consider giving them, say, an inexpensive contact-management package for a trial period. From that will flow suggestions for a more custom-designed system to meet their needs.

- *Make the system easy to learn and use.* Of utmost importance is the user interface that guides sales reps through the system. Also, the various screens should resemble the paper forms of your manual lead-tracking system.

- *Provide training and support.* Make sure every salesperson knows how to use the system, and provide phone support for field reps. Colombo notes that Condé Nast, the magazine publisher, broke the ice for computer neophytes by introducing the system with a game and typing lessons.

# 278
## IDEA

# Face-to-Face, Almost

**D**o your salespeople hop on and off airplanes as much as most people get in and out of bed? **Videoconferencing may be the answer** to your sales expense-account woes. Proponents say that phone calls combined with video images provide a money-saving alternative to business travel.

For less than $2,000, you can equip your PC with the software, video board, camera, and phone lines you need to hold a videoconference with a similarly equipped party, says Kenyon Hayward, president of V-SPAN, a teleconferencing network services provider in Wayne, Pa. Vendors such as Apple, Polycom, Creative Labs, Intel, and PictureTel sell videoconferencing kits, or you can experiment with videoconferencing without making a big investment by renting the services of a copy center. For example, Kinko's, a business services chain, rents videoconferencing facilities in more than 100 of its locations starting at $150 an hour.

Susan Smith, a principal at Service Intelligence, a $3-million market-research firm in Seattle that serves clients such as Starbucks Coffee, Westin Hotels, and Norwest Bank, typically stages one- or two-hour videoconferences at nearby copy shops. Participants in the Service Intelligence videoconferences can see and talk to one another. They can also look at and mark up proposals, color bar charts, even photographs. The cost? Field agents in Miami, New York, and San Francisco were linked up in a two-hour videoconference for $1,500. The same task done the old-fashioned way would have cost $6,000 in travel expenses and taken 40 hours.

For a listing of videoconferencing facilities, call the International Teleconferencing Association at 610-941-2020.

## XI

"For every 20 calls you place,
you'll actually speak to 15 people.
Seven of those will ask you to
follow up with a second call, and
of those, 2 or 3 will be prospects,
and one will buy."

**STEPHAN SCHIFFMAN**
sales trainer, DEI Management Group,
New York, N.Y.

**279**

**IDEA**

# Time Warp

The floral delivery company 1-800-FLOWERS was often inundated by phone calls, particularly during holiday periods. In his book *Stop and Smell the Roses* (Ballantine, 1998, $25), president Jim McCann reports that customers of his $300-million Westbury, N.Y., company were irritated when their calls were not answered by the third ring. He also knew that customers disliked being put on hold.

The solution? **Lengthening the time between phone rings from six to nine seconds.** The change gave operators more time to answer the phone by the third ring. When interviewed, customers reported that they didn't notice the lengthened ringing cycle. And the solution cost virtually nothing.

**280**
**IDEA**

# Back to the Future

One of the most important responsibilities that you have to your customers—and one of the best ways of assuring that they remain yours—is to treat them like human beings. A voice-mail system that bounces customers from one automated menu to the next is a sure way to make them feel like extremely frustrated robots.

A poll taken by the folks at Keena Mfg., in Brunswick, Maine, showed that its customers had an overwhelming distaste for voice mail. "The reason was simple," explains Harvey Epstein, owner of the $3-million packing-tape manufacturer. "Human contact is lost in a sea of electronic menus, thwarting instant gratification."

And so, the company that created Sizzltape, an innovative packaging tape that's laminated with high-quality gift wrap, rejected voice mail—even though it could have been installed for just a few dollars a month. To avoid the caller backup that sometimes occurs—since the 15-person company doesn't employ a receptionist—there is a pecking order of **employees answering lines as they light up**. The phones are not allowed to ring more than twice before a customer-service rep answers and promptly dispenses information or takes an order. "We even instruct the reps in the art of schmoozing—'How's the weather?' 'How was your vacation?'—something voice mail can't do," Epstein says.

# 281
## IDEA

# Voice Mail on a Grand Scale

To recruit new customers, Lens Express advertises heavily, both in print and on television. Menderes Akdag, president of the $53-million mail-order contact-lens company in Deerfield Beach, Fla., used to hire a telemarketing firm staffed with operators to field calls generated by his TV ads. But the firm's reports showed that 30% to 40% of the people who dialed the Lens Express 800 number were getting busy signals.

Akdag first experimented with an automated voice-response system for the overflow calls. Although he was initially wary of directing potential customers to an automated menu, he discovered that the switch didn't affect response rates. Then he tried using **automated voice response to answer all the advertising-generated calls**—and found that he could save 40% to 50%. Now people who call the Lens Express 800 number get a menu inviting them to "press 1 for a free brochure, press 2 to order from a Lens Express operator." According to Akdag, 88% of the callers want the brochure and don't need to talk to a human being.

Because the automated system can handle thousands of calls at once, Akdag says he no longer has busy-signal problems. He considered the automated voice-response services offered by telemarketing companies and other long-distance providers, but in the end he chose his long-distance carrier. One factor: The phone-call volume that once accrued to the telemarketing firm now counts as Lens Express's, so the company can qualify for a lower phone rate based on volume.

**IDEA**

# Don't Miss a Call

**E**very evening at closing time, the six answering machines at Magellan's kicked in. And each morning the machines played back partial orders and messages saying, "I'm not leaving my credit-card number on an answering machine!" John McManus, CEO of this travel-supplies mail-order house in Santa Barbara, Calif., could only guess how many potential customers hung up.

Then McManus discovered the AT&T Merlin Legend, **an automated answering and order-taking system**, which has voice prompts that ask callers for their name, address, credit-card number, item number, and quantity. He signed a $45,000, five-year contract (today, he says, he'd insist on a year-to-year contract) that covers a dozen phone lines—taking not only calls throughout the night but also overflow calls during the day. That was a good deal, because staffing for the overflow coverage alone would have taken two more employees at a cost of at least $32,000 a year.

The day after the system was installed, McManus knew he'd made the right investment. Previously, Magellan's would receive some 20 messages during the night—mostly catalog requests and "a brave few orders." But the first morning with the new system, McManus counted more than 200 messages, with a higher percentage of orders than usual. That ratio has stayed high: Now, about 35% of all calls are orders, up from 10% during the old answering-machine days. And Magellan's order rate once hit an industry high—about 40%.

**283**

**IDEA**

# Two-Tier Telemarketing

**W**ith only a $5,000 product to offer, CWC Software, in Braintree, Mass., can't afford to put a salesperson on the road. So the 15-year-old company—which sells a subscription-fulfillment program called QuickFill—makes strategic use of its telemarketing, **dividing the responsibilities of its phone sales force so that one person is a "prospector" and one is a "closer."**

The prospector is a less expensive part-timer who doesn't need detailed product knowledge or finely honed selling skills. The prospector makes the initial contact with people who respond to CWC ads. "He can make sure that prospects received the demo disk they ask for," says vice-president Bill Bean, "and encourage them to open it and try it." The prospector also answers the most commonly asked questions.

Companies on CWC's long list receive quarterly newsletters and periodic calls. When prospects start to look like buyers, their names go onto the "hot" list. The seasoned closer—an experienced salesperson with extensive product knowledge—answers specific questions and lobbies everyone at the prospect's company who must approve the purchase.

Using this two-tiered approach, CWC has steadily increased its sales by about 20% each year to $1.5 million in 1997. Some telemarketers, however, believe you should have two closers for every prospector. For now Bean is content to see the company in the black and meeting sales projections.

**284**

**IDEA**

# Prepared for Anything

**M**ost prospects have nagging doubts about working with a company over the phone. Eliminating those doubts is our challenge," says Ashok Trivedi, founder and president of Mastech, a Pittsburgh-based provider of temporary software programmers.

Mastech **does its homework for telesales pitches diligently**, just as if a representative were meeting the prospect in person. The company systematically gathers information on potential clients from exclusive industry research firms, trade publications, customer referrals, and news from its front-line scouts: 3,000 full-time employees working around the world. Thus, Mastech telemarketers can dazzle skeptical prospects with knowledge of their needs and how Mastech can fill them.

To outdo competitors, Mastech salespeople follow up within hours of a call. They fax profiles on programmers suitable for the prospect's project, their rates, and a list of references—customers in the region with whom Mastech has worked. The list also includes the names of other customers in the prospect's industry. These measures help build trust with prospects, despite the lack of personal contact. "At the end of the day, we must deliver on what we promise," says Trivedi. "That's how you really build rapport." Judging by the company's accounts, Mastech has met that challenge. In 1997, it rang up $195 million in sales, more than 50% of which were closed over the phone.

"In talking with people, keep emphasizing the things on which you agree. Get the person saying, 'yes, yes,' at the outset. As much as possible, keep him from saying 'no.' When a person has said no, all his pride and personality demands that he remain consistent with himself."

**DALE CARNEGIE**
author, *How to Win Friends and Influence People* (Simon & Schuster)

**285**

**IDEA**

# Playing Well with Others

In-house telemarketing, a solid source of qualified leads and sales, can also become a battlefield between phone and field salespeople. "Lots of cannibalizing of sales," says Rudy Schlacher, referring to the infighting that once divided his eight in-house telemarketers and 18 independent field sales reps at Washburn International, a $58-million guitar maker in Vernon Hills, Ill.

CEO Schlacher got field and phone reps to work in harmony by **rewarding collective efforts**. Under Washburn's old system, phone reps received a commission of 1% to 1.5% only on the instruments they sold. As the guitar industry changed (shorter sales cycles, more phone-in orders from music stores), telemarketers played a more pivotal role in helping field salespeople maintain old accounts and open new ones. So Schlacher now pays phone reps an extra 0.75% commission on field sales made in their territory; outside salespeople still get a commission of 6% to 8%. Thanks to assistance from the phone reps, outside salespeople now have more time to focus on introducing new products and holding in-store clinics.

The added cost of Washburn's revised commission plan is a small percentage of the 9% sales increase reaped since the change. "The salespeople aren't fighting anymore," says Schlacher. "There's real teamwork."

**286**
**IDEA**

# Show and Sell on the Web

Jim Schwertner, president of Capitol Land and Livestock, has improved his telemarketing staff's productivity thanks to clever use of the World Wide Web. Every day, Schwertner's cattle-brokering business, which has about 100 employees, buys 1,500 head of cattle at auctions and trucks them back to headquarters in Schwertner, Tex. (named for his great-grandfather). By day's end, all 1,500 are gone—sold by five telemarketers, in lots of about 100 animals each, to ranchers and feed yards.

In the past, those salespeople had to spend several minutes of each call describing the day's offerings to cattle buyers. Now Schwertner's **telemarketers let customers do their own visual inspection on the company's Web site**, which contains enlargeable photos of each of the lots of cattle. Schwertner's controller takes the photos each morning using a digital camera.

Schwertner says that about a third of his company's 400 regular clients refer to the Web site during calls. And Schwertner's staff members find that they can close their Web-supported sales calls within roughly half the customary time. The time they save is important because the company turns its inventory every day; as a result, Capitol Land and Livestock can generally get better prices if its salespeople can reach more prospects.

# 287
## IDEA

# Four Ways to Test Teleprospecting

**U**sing the phone to sell a product or service is relatively inexpensive. So whether you're doing the calling in-house or hiring a service, you can afford to **experiment with telesales**. Here are four ideas from Jack Falvey, managing director of Intermark, a small Londonderry, N.H., consulting firm.

1. *Introduce mail with the phone.* Call people to ask them to watch for material you've mailed, or ask their permission to send it. Mailing to willing recipients saves postage and gives you a better-qualified lead.

2. *Follow up a mailing with a phone call.* The mailing should include a response vehicle, such as a postcard to send back or a number to call. But making a follow-up call can double your response.

3. *Conduct a market survey.* Use the phone to learn what features or benefits that customers value in the product or service you propose to sell. Or use your calls to test a price.

4. *Conduct an after-market survey.* Call customers to find out if you met their expectations. Doing this during a market test will give you an indication of what your long-term success will be.

# 288
## IDEA

# Dialing for Dollars

**M**agazine subscriptions at $12 a year can sell over the telephone, but what about the services of a software programmer costing $100,000? Ashok Trivedi figured it was worth the cost of a few phone calls to find out. When his company, Mastech, was a cash-strapped start-up, it could not afford branch offices to serve major corporations in their local areas. So Trivedi needed to differentiate his company from the competition. One way to do that was to **use telesales instead of branch offices**. Selling by phone allowed Mastech to pass on savings to its customers and bid more competitively for work.

Telemarketing has since enabled the Pittsburgh-based company to extend its sales territories to places like Battle Creek, Mich., and Wichita, where competitors' branch offices don't reach and where demand for programmers familiar with leading-edge software can far exceed supply. As a result, prospects are more willing to listen to a sales pitch over the phone, since they are more in need of the service. Now more than 50% of Mastech's $195 million in sales come from its in-house phone reps.

**289 IDEA**

# Heat Up Cold Calls

Cold calling is a hard sell. But not if you call the right people. Carmela Daniele has **built a successful business using chamber of commerce lists**. Daniele, owner of A Gift Basket by Carmela, in Springfield, Mass., creates custom gift baskets full of gourmet Italian foods, desserts, drinks, and personal products. She started the company in 1992 in her basement and began cold calling. "Quite a few people hung up on me," she recalls.

Then she joined her local chamber of commerce and the Italy-America Chamber of Commerce, in New York City, and began to call the business owners on their lists. Daniele found that by identifying herself as a fellow member, many people would hear her out. That's when she started to get orders. A local Nissan dealer, who thought she was crazy when she suggested he send a basket to each new buyer, ended up liking the idea because it set him apart. Now he orders 2,000 baskets a year.

"I've tried direct mail, brochures, faxes," says Daniele, "but my response rate for cold calls is much higher. Sure, it takes time, but I have a headset and just talk while I'm making baskets. My phone bills were outrageous in the beginning—$600 to $700 a month—but I've got one client alone who orders several thousand dollars of baskets each Christmas." Daniele now works from a warehouse, employs 10 people part-time, and is opening a big store on Springfield's Main Street.

**290**
**IDEA**

# Traffic Code

**Y**our telemarketers may be top closers, but do they heed the **Federal Trade Commission's Telemarketing Sales Rule**? The rule cracks down on abusive telemarketing practices, such as calling consumers at home who have asked not to be called a second time. While targeted at consumer telemarketers, the rule also affects business-to-business marketers of nondurable office goods such as pencils, paper, printer toner, and cleaning supplies.

To help companies follow the regulations, the Direct Marketing Association joined forces with the Federal Trade Commission to produce *Complying with the Telemarketing Sales Rule* and a pamphlet, *A Business Checklist for Direct Marketers*, which provides an overview of several FTC rules. For free single copies, contact the Direct Marketing Association's consumer-affairs office by fax at 202-955-0085, or write to 1111 19th St. NW, Suite 1100, Washington, D.C. 20036.

**XII**

"If you're not doing something different, why should anyone buy from you? There are many companies in the field. Many are larger with more resources, and you have to compete with them in the mailbox. You have to find a way to stand out and gain your own identity."

**JOHN PETERMAN**
founder and owner, J. Peterman Co.,
Lexington, Ky.

# 291
**IDEA**

## Sizing Up Satisfaction

**S**oliciting feedback from customers is only the first step toward improving customer relations. Once you've gotten the feedback, what do you do with it? Rather than issuing a report or a memo that gets shuffled across employees' desks and then gets lost, take some advice from $35-million WinterSilks. The Middleton, Wis., mail-order company **distributes a monthly list of the top 10 customer comments, both good and bad, to all staff members**.

The top-10 list helps employees recognize simple ways to increase customer satisfaction. For example, if several customers complain that a certain blouse fits too tightly around the shoulders, customer-service representatives can advise callers to order a larger size if they are buying it for a broad-shouldered person. Giving the customer unexpected help increases phone rapport, boosting the likelihood of repeat business.

**292**
**IDEA**

# Close-Knit Cooperation

**A** typical retail buyer tends to assume that, if a company's marketing literature looks first-rate, then its product line is too. Dia, a small manufacturer of hand-knit chenille sweaters sold to exclusive women's boutiques nationwide, managed to keep up a stylish appearance by **joining forces with retailers to produce a tasteful catalog** of its sweaters every year.

"Stores began to request extra copies of our catalog. We found out they were giving them to undecided and time-starved shoppers," says John Leehman, CEO of the Vergennes, Vt., company. "So we gave them an opportunity to order the catalog in bulk, at $1 apiece, then used the funds to finance a second print run. Everybody wins: We defray the $10,000 cost of publishing the catalog, and the retailers get a better marketing piece than they could afford to put together themselves."

Dia's tactic also translates into increased sales: It's a $4-million company growing by 25% a year.

# Blueprint for Buyers

**C**atalogs from Design Basics, a home-plan publisher based in Omaha, once grouped home designs primarily by architectural style. Although this organization was logical to architects and builders, it didn't make the most sense to prospective home buyers. So the company **redesigned its product literature to reflect the needs of its customers**.

President Linda Reimer discovered that home buyers are more interested in how a house functions than in its style; they were juggling a number of catalogs to find the few pages in each that fit their needs. Design Basics took the cue and now publishes a series of four home-design books called "Seasons." The new catalogs emphasize functional features appropriate for different age groups and geographic regions. For instance, a young family would look at "Spring," which features homes outfitted with mud rooms and nurseries; empty nesters can peruse the "Winter" volume to find designs with master bedrooms on the main floor and fewer stairs.

Departing from standard industry practice is paying off. "Anything that helps prospects make up their minds—and decide specifically on a Design Basics home rather than one from a competitor—is worth the effort," says Reimer. Reorganizing the catalog cost about 25% more than a typical update, but 1997 orders for home plans from these books came in 50% faster than those from previous catalogs.

**294**

**IDEA**

# Post Haste

To sell Intelimed, a new computer system that provides doctors with status reports on clinical lab work, Michael Lillig consulted a group of prospective customers. They surprised him by saying that a postcard would be more effective than face-to-face sales calls or a four-color accordion-pleated brochure. Among busy doctors and nurses, "I had 30 seconds of a prospect's time" to convey the message, says Lillig, vice-president of sales and marketing for Quantum Laboratories, in Seattle. The results within three months of mailing 2,100 postcards: $300,000 in orders.

With just seconds to get a recipient's attention, the copy on the postcard is crucial. Copywriters swear by the AIDA formula—Attention, Interest, Desire, Action. A direct-mail piece should contain all four elements, says Lillig, but "the call to action—such as 'Call Today!'—is very important." Lillig also relied on some other **copywriting basics**. Here's a sampling:

◆ *Use power words.* Single words such as "announcing," "free," "innovation," "special," "guarantee," and "savings" get noticed. Short, direct questions such as "How?" and "Interested?" are also attention-grabbers.

◆ *Keep it simple.* Lillig aimed his text at a seventh- to eighth-grade reading level because experts say more people will read simple copy.

◆ *Use bullets.* Bullets make it easy to pick out important points.

◆ *Repeat yourself.* Lillig put "Intelimed" in caps and repeated the name nine times to help prospects remember it.

◆ *Use P.S. footnotes.* These are the most-read part of any printed page. P.S. footnotes should support the headline, not the body text. In Lillig's postscript, "no charge" took readers back to the headline word "free."

# Drumming Up Business

To get to know the people who ultimately use its products, Pro-Mark, a premier drumstick maker in Houston, made its magazine advertising more interactive by **offering free product samples in return for customer feedback**. The first campaign generated more than 3,000 responses. The respondents' names were entered into a database, and each received a catalog in addition to the sample drumsticks. The new test marketers have proved to be conscientious reviewers. For example, when Pro-Mark recently tested a new finish, it sent samples to 125 drummers, and only one failed to return the detailed questionnaire. For the first two years of the project, the company boasted a 100% response rate.

Another ad announced a contest for the "Not-Yet-Famous Drummer." Readers sent in photos of themselves along with a survey card, indicating preferences in drumsticks, music styles, and bands—information that helps the company target future promotions. Pro-Mark doubled its database as 5,000 people entered the contest, and photos of the winners appeared in subsequent ads.

The company also added another 3,500 names to its list by having coupons double as raffle tickets. In addition to getting a pair of sticks for $5, readers became eligible to win a chance to hang out with Dave Abbruzzese, the former Pearl Jam drummer.

# 296
**IDEA**

## Everything's Coming Up Roses

**P**rior to the winter planting season, Burkard Nurseries mails its yearly rose catalog, which lists more than 500 collectible roses, to 16,000 customers in the Pasadena, Calif., area. "Even if they don't buy a rose, it helps remind them to visit Burkard the next time they need a plant," says Frank Burkard. "The catalog also has a long shelf life. I've seen people come in with tattered copies six months later to see if we still have an item."

Although just 7% of its customers are avid rose gardeners, the catalog is a money-maker for the company—it sells between $40,000 and $50,000 worth of bare root roses annually and costs just $10,000 to produce. To squeeze more out of its rose catalog, Burkard **supplements that niche-oriented promotional piece with items that have more general appeal**.

"We don't have a big marketing budget, so we have to get as much out of it as possible. Now we include a page promoting our Christmas trees, poinsettias, and potted arrangements. Last year, we included fruit trees and a blueberry bush that grows in Southern California. We did a couple of thousand dollars in fruit trees alone," beams Burkard. The primary focus on roses helps the company distinguish itself from lower-end retailers and discount stores, and the new items have made new sales blossom.

# Going Postal

**C**leaning up a direct-mail list is one of those business chores that isn't a high priority with many companies. That can mean slow delivery for already slow bulk-rate mailers. What's more, mailing pieces that don't meet post-office size guidelines get slapped with a five-cent surcharge.

As a one-time free service, the approximately 100 Postal Business Centers around the country will take your mailing list (up to 50,000 names), insert the correct postal bar codes, and standardize the addresses. Contact a design analyst at your nearest Postal Business Center, and ask for the free guide, The Small Business Guide to Advertising with Direct Mail, to **make sure your mailers conform to postal requirements**. You can also incorporate the bar codes using a program such as "My Professional Mail Manager," from MySoftware (800-325-9095). Either way, you'll probably qualify for the post office's automation discount.

# 298
## IDEA

# Our Price Includes Answers

**F**axes have become the secret to smarter selling for UV Process Supply, a Chicago mail-order firm that sells technical supplies to companies that use ultraviolet light in printing. When customers had equipment problems, they used to call president and CEO Stephen Siegel, an industry veteran with more than 20 years' experience. That was great for them but not so great for Siegel, who often spent one-third of his day taking calls. Siegel estimates that his time on the phone has since been reduced by about 85%, thanks to extensive use of a fax-on-demand program. Customers calling the **fax-on-demand service** can choose from hundreds of documents that cover all kinds of technical questions.

UV Process Supply, which does about $5 million a year in sales, has integrated the service into its catalog: Each product description includes instructions for obtaining additional information by fax. Most of the documents in UV's database are product-information files that the company developed, so they already reside on UV's local area network. Others—such as product instruction manuals—must be scanned in.

Using the fax-on-demand service costs UV's customers nothing, except for the toll call. That's because Siegel views the information the company provides as an integral part of its sales process, largely replacing a sales and technical-support staff. At first, it was hard to coax customers to try his service, but at its peak, the system averaged a healthy 20 calls a day, and all but the most technophobic customers used it. Although the fax-back system is still operating, most customers now field their tech questions through UV Process Supply's Web site.

# Turn Expo Goers into Prospects

I f a trade show or expo doesn't publish the names of attendees, **contact the event's promoter to obtain the registration list**—it's a prime source of new sales leads. The lists can be sliced and diced to suit your specific needs. Take it from Michael Hough, conference producer of A/E/C Systems International, in Exton, Pa., who relies on his own company's database to pitch showgoers on the possibility of attending another show.

Hough narrows his list of attendees—primarily architects and engineers interested in computer equipment—down to only the most promising prospects to create promotions tailored to their interests. Using a FoxPro database of 50,000 names, he sends out 30 to 40 mailings, or 500,000 pieces a year, based on specific criteria. Most letters are processed by an outside mail house, which offers a bulk-mail discount of about 2¢ apiece. Hough gives the mail house a disk with names, addresses, and attributes, along with instructions about which attributes to combine and which letters to send to which combinations.

Thanks to Hough's systematic approach, conference revenues continue to go up: In 1997, they topped $821,000.

# Mini-Promos Pack a Punch

**N**atural Ovens of Manitowoc, in Manitowoc, Wis., packs a one-page newsletter with every loaf of bread. Pete's Brewing, in Palo Alto, Calif., tucked a minicatalog into each six-pack. Call them **"guided missives" that reach customers when they are most receptive**—with savings on postage and production as additional benefits.

Natural Ovens prints its newsletter on the flip side of its bread label, which is folded lengthwise inside the loaf's plastic bag. Each week's issue includes health tips, recipes, and letters from consumers. "Thousands of people called in response to the newsletter," reports Barbara Stitt, co-owner and president of the bakery, which sells to 1,400 supermarkets. Increasing the label size to fit the newsletter raised costs by only one-half cent per loaf, but overall, printing the newsletter on the label saved $1,000 an issue.

In a bookmark-size catalog that unfolded to 13 inches, Pete's Brewing told beer lovers about its "Wicked Ware," a sideline of T-shirts and mugs. The catalog listed an 800 number, and within two years it generated 1,200 orders a month.

# Traveling First Class

**D**espite the expense, sending your direct mail **first class instead of bulk rate** can be worth it, particularly for high-end promotions, says Bob Nelson, founder and president of Nelson Motivation, a management training and consulting firm in San Diego. "First class increases your audience, and it gives you control over delivery," he says. "You know exactly when recipients are going to get the mail, and you can be pretty sure they're going to open it, especially if the envelope has a first-class stamp."

Nelson is a speaker for the two-time *Inc.* 500 company Wyncom, a producer of high-end business seminars. He says that Wyncom runs about 175 programs a year in cities throughout the United States and sends out about 50,000 direct-mail pieces per program—all via first-class mail.

Wyncom reports that first class is successful because it generates strong seminar registration and provides a mechanism for tracking the exact number of people who received the mailing. First-class mail also makes it easier to keep mailing lists up to date because information about incorrect or changed addresses is returned to the sender.

As for return on investment, Nelson offers the following formula: At a cost of about $1 per piece (first-class postage, envelope, address label, marketing literature), you'll spend $1,000 per 1,000 names. If 1% of recipients respond (a reasonable response) and spend an average of $100, the gross will be $1,000—the amount of your direct-mail outlay. "If you have high-quality products or services and know specifically who could best benefit from them, there's no better way to go," Nelson concludes.

• INDEX • INDEX •

**301 GREAT IDEAS FOR SELLING SMARTER**

Other business books from *Inc.* magazine

**HOW TO *REALLY* CREATE A SUCCESSFUL BUSINESS PLAN**
**HOW TO *REALLY* CREATE A SUCCESSFUL MARKETING PLAN**
**HOW TO *REALLY* START YOUR OWN BUSINESS**
By David E. Gumpert

**MANAGING PEOPLE**
**HOW TO *REALLY* RECRUIT, MOTIVATE, AND LEAD YOUR TEAM**
Edited by Ruth G. Newman
with Bradford W. Ketchum, Jr.

**HOW TO *REALLY* DELIVER SUPERIOR CUSTOMER SERVICE**
Edited by John Halbrooks

**THE SERVICE BUSINESS PLANNING GUIDE**
By Warren G. Purdy

**THE GUIDE TO RETAIL BUSINESS PLANNING**
By Warren G. Purdy

**MANAGING PEOPLE: 101 PROVEN IDEAS FOR MAKING**
**YOU AND YOUR PEOPLE MORE PRODUCTIVE**
**FROM AMERICA'S SMARTEST SMALL COMPANIES**
Edited by Sara P. Noble

**301 GREAT MANAGEMENT IDEAS**
**FROM AMERICA'S MOST INNOVATIVE SMALL COMPANIES**
Edited by Leslie Brokaw

**301 DO-IT-YOURSELF MARKETING IDEAS**
**FROM AMERICA'S MOST INNOVATIVE SMALL COMPANIES**
Edited by Sam Decker

**301 GREAT CUSTOMER SERVICE IDEAS**
**FROM AMERICA'S MOST INNOVATIVE SMALL COMPANIES**
Edited by Nancy Artz

**301 GREAT IDEAS FOR USING TECHNOLOGY**
**FROM AMERICA'S MOST INNOVATIVE SMALL COMPANIES**
Edited by Phaedra Hise

**www.inc.com/products**

To receive a complete listing of *Inc.* business books and videos, please call 1-800-468-0800, ext. 5505. Or write to *Inc.* Business Resources, P.O. Box 1365, Dept. 5505, Wilkes-Barre, PA 18703-1365.